ROUTLEDGE LIBRARY EDITIONS: JAPANESE LINGUISTICS

Volume 3

INTERACTION OF DERIVATIONAL MORPHOLOGY AND SYNTAX IN JAPANESE AND ENGLISH

INTERACTION OF DERIVATIONAL MORPHOLOGY AND SYNTAX IN JAPANESE AND ENGLISH

YOKO SUGIOKA

Routledge
Taylor & Francis Group
LONDON AND NEW YORK

First published in 1986 by Garland Publishing, Inc.

This edition first published in 2019
by Routledge
2 Park Square, Milton Park, Abingdon, Oxon OX14 4RN

and by Routledge
52 Vanderbilt Avenue, New York, NY 10017

Routledge is an imprint of the Taylor & Francis Group, an informa business

© 1985 Yoko Sugioka

All rights reserved. No part of this book may be reprinted or reproduced or utilised in any form or by any electronic, mechanical, or other means, now known or hereafter invented, including photocopying and recording, or in any information storage or retrieval system, without permission in writing from the publishers.

Trademark notice: Product or corporate names may be trademarks or registered trademarks, and are used only for identification and explanation without intent to infringe.

British Library Cataloguing in Publication Data
A catalogue record for this book is available from the British Library

ISBN: 978-1-138-36949-8 (Set)
ISBN: 978-0-429-40043-8 (Set) (ebk)
ISBN: 978-0-367-00174-2 (Volume 3) (hbk)
ISBN: 978-0-367-00187-2 (Volume 3) (pbk)
ISBN: 978-0-429-40093-3 (Volume 3) (ebk)

Publisher's Note
The publisher has gone to great lengths to ensure the quality of this reprint but points out that some imperfections in the original copies may be apparent.

Disclaimer
The publisher has made every effort to trace copyright holders and would welcome correspondence from those they have been unable to trace.

Interaction of Derivational Morphology and Syntax in Japanese and English

Yoko Sugioka

Garland Publishing, Inc. ▪ New York & London
1986

Library of Congress Cataloging-in-Publication Data

Sugioka, Yoko.
  Interaction of derivational morphology and syntax in Japanese and English.

  (Outstanding dissertations in linguistics)
  Originally presented as the author's thesis (Ph.D.)—University of Chicago, 1984.
  Bibliography: p.
  1. Japanese language—Morphology. 2. Japanese language—Syntax. 3. English language—Morphology. 4. English language—Syntax. 5. Lexicology. I. Title. II. Series.
PL559.S8 1986   425   85-31112
ISBN 0-8240-5478-4 (alk. paper)

© 1985 by Yoko Sugioka
All Rights Reserved

The volumes in this series are printed on acid-free, 250-year-life paper.

Printed in the United States of America

THE UNIVERSITY OF CHICAGO

INTERACTION OF DERIVATIONAL MORPHOLOGY AND SYNTAX
IN JAPANESE AND ENGLISH

A DISSERTATION SUBMITTED TO
THE FACULTY OF THE DIVISION OF HUMANITIES
IN CANDIDACY FOR THE DEGREE OF
DOCTOR OF PHILOSOPHY

DEPARTMENT OF LINGUISTICS

BY
YOKO SUGIOKA

CHICAGO, ILLINOIS
DECEMBER, 1984

ACKNOWLEDGEMENTS

I wish first to express my profound gratitude to the members of my committee, Jim McCawley, Jerry Sadock, and Bill Darden, for guiding me through the various stages of the dissertation research and writing. Throughout my graduate education at the University of Chicago I have benefited enormously from the numerous courses on various subjects and a number of reading sessions I took from Jim McCawley. His persistent enthusiasm and insightful approaches in tackling many problems of linguistics taught me a great deal about what it is to be a linguist. During the time of my dissertation writing, Jim was consistently encouraging and helpful. I am truly thankful for all this. I am especially grateful to Jerry Sadock for the enormous help he gave in shaping this dissertation. The basic theoretical framework of this dissertation developed first out of the reading sessions I had with Jerry. He also influenced me a great deal through his past and ongoing work on Greenlandic and the morphology/syntax interaction. I cannot thank him enough for the detailed criticisms and consistent encouragements he offered me on the earlier versions of each chapter. I am also grateful to Bill Darden for the insightful comments on the earlier version of this work, as well as for the help he gave me as the chairman of the department.

I would like to thank the faculty and my fellow students at the Department of Linguistics of the University of Chicago for providing such a warm and cozy environment to study in. I owe big thanks to Rachel Lehr, my special friend, who discussed with me many of the issues brought up in this dissertation and provided me with such a great friendship whenever I needed it. I am also grateful to Ann Wehmeyer for reading and correcting the manuscripts as well as for lots of encouragements. I also wish to thank Donka Farkas, Kat Momoi, John Richardson, and Rob Chametzky for stimulating discussion on various linguistic subjects and moral support. Finally, I would like to thank my non-linguist friends in Hyde Park for making my life here so much more enjoyable and meaningful.

The following institutions and organizations provided me with financial support during my graduate study at Chicago: the Division of Humanities of the University of Chicago, the Center for Far Eastern Studies of the University of Chicago, Rotary International, P.E.O. International, American Association of University Women, Kobe College Alumni Association. I am deeply grateful for their financial help, without which I could not have completed my graduate work at Chicago.

Finally, I wish to express my deep gratitude to my parents, Tomio and Setsuko Sugioka, and my husband, Kazuo Todokoro, for their consistent support, both mental and material.

TABLE OF CONTENTS

	Page
ACKNOWLEDGEMENTS	i
INTRODUCTION	1

Chapter

I. SOME THEORETICAL ISSUES 4

    1. The syntax/lexicon dichotomy--The
       development of the Lexicalist
       Hypothesis 4
    2. Word Formation Rules 8
       2.1. Rule Formalisms 9
       2.2. Level ordering and Adjacency
           Condition 13
       2.3. Head 17
       2.4. Inflection vs. Derivation 19
       2.5. Semantics of Word 21
    3. Typology of rules 26
       3.1. Earlier attempts for rule typology . . . 26
       3.2. Rule vs. operation: Dowty's (1979)
           proposal 27
       3.3. Interaction of processes 30
       3.4. Cliticization 42
    4. Lexicalism in Japanese Syntax 47

II. DEVERBAL NOMINALS AND COMPOUNDS 56

    1. English verbal compounds and argument
       structure 56
       1.1. First Sister Principle 56
       1.2. Verbal compounds vs. primary
           compounds 58
       1.3. An alternative analysis of verbal
           compounds 64
       1.4. No subject condition 72
       1.5. The generic condition on the
           realization of the argument
           structure 73
    2. Deverbal nominals and compounds in
       Japanese 77
       2.1. Deverbal compounds 79
       2.2. Suffixed deverbal nominals 93
    3. A note on the condition on rendaku 105

III. ARGUMENT STRUCTURE AND DERIVATIONAL MORPHOLOGY
    OF ADJECTIVES 114

    1. Argument structure of English adjectives . 115
        1.1. Complement inheritance under
             nominalization 116
        1.2. Adjectival compounds 123
    2. Nominalization of Japanese adjectives . . . 126
        2.1. Two types of nominalizing suffixes . . 126
        2.2. Argument structure and case marking
             of adjectives 130
        2.3. Complements under nominalization . . . 132
        2.4. Extended domain of the nominalization . 137
    3. On the verbalizing suffix -garu 146

IV. PHRASAL SUFFIXES I: ALTERNATING CASE MARKING . . 153

    1. Phrasal suffixation and reanalysis 153
    2. Facts about Japanese stative predicate
       constructions 155
    3. Proposal 158
    4. Morphological transparency 161
    5. Conditions for the reanalysis 165
        5.1. Distance between the second NP and
             the predicate 165
        5.2. Conjunction and comparatives 167
        5.3. The distance between the verb and
             -tai 172
        5.4. Semantic conditions 173
    6. Concluding remarks and some issues 176
        6.1. Basic and derived case patterns for
             stative predicates 176
        6.2. On the object-hood of the second NP . . 181
        6.3. The accusative NP condition--a
             problem 184

V. PHRASAL SUFFIXES II 190

    1. Suffixes with phrasal scopes 191
        1.1. Reciprocal suffix -au 191
        1.2. On the suffix -sugiru 199
    2. Nominal forming suffixes 209
        2.1. Adjectival nominal forming suffixes . . 209
        2.2. Predicate nominal forming suffixes . . 211
    3. Subordinate clause suffixes 214
    4. The domain of passive suffixation 220

VI. CONCLUDING REMARKS 229

BIBLIOGRAPHY 237

INTRODUCTION

The main issue that is addressed in this thesis is the question of how the proper boundary between the lexicon and syntax should be defined. In this respect, various word formation processes in Japanese and English which seem to involve some interaction of morphology and syntax are examined here.

In the past 15 years of studies on the lexicon and word formation we saw a development of so-called Lexicalism, starting with Chomsky's 'Remarks on Nominalization', followed by various works by people such as Aronoff, Siegel, Allen, Lieber, Selkirk, Kiparsky and so on. In these works it is maintained that word formation belongs only to the lexicon and does not systematically interact with syntactic rules. In other words, morphology, which involves sub-word-level derivations, is never fed by syntax, which involves phrase and sentence level derivations. Even though this view creates relatively few problems for English word formation, that is not the case with typologically different languages. For instance, noun incorporation in West Greenlandic, a polysynthetic language, has been claimed to be syntactic by Sadock (1980). As an agglutinative language, Japanese should serve as a good testing ground for the universality of the Lexicalism. There have been, however, only a few studies done in this respect, and further more, the lexicalist claims about Japanese (or arguments against them) have pretty much been limited to such constructions as passives and causatives, which have been well discussed in syntactic analyses.[1] Thus one major purpose of this dissertation is to examine a wide range of word formation processes in Japanese and question the plausibility of the lexicalist hypothesis as a theory of universal grammar.

The organization of this dissertation is as the following. In Chapter I the development of the lexicalist hypothesis and the various specific claims and assumptions made in regard to word formation processes are discussed, after which a rule typology approach to the syntax/lexicon dichotomy is proposed as a framework of this dissertation. In Chapter II we look at deverbal nominals and compounds in English and Japanese, and discuss their similarities and differences. Chapter III will deal with nominalization and verbalization of adjectives in the two languages and discuss in particular the important role argument structure plays in morphological derivations. Chapter IV takes up one specific consequence of the framework proposed here, namely the

---

[1] One notable exception is Kageyama (1982), and a number of claims he makes are discussed in many places of this dissertation.

possibility of phrasal suffixation, and apply it to the analysis of the derived stative predicate constructions in Japanese. In Chapter V, other suffixes with phrasal scope are discussed, and some of them are compared to the English affixes with similar functions. The observations made in these chapters are summarized in Chapter VI.

CHAPTER I

SOME THEORETICAL ISSUES

This chapter provides the basic background for the theoretical issues in the treatment of the role of the lexicon in grammar and the properties of word formation in general. In Section 1 we will briefly discuss the development of 'lexicalism' concerning the boundary between syntax and the lexicon. In Section 2 we will discuss a number of claims that have been made about the properties of word formation and the organization of the lexicon; some of them are specifically for English, but many of them are supposed to hold across languages. Some problems for those claims will be discussed. Then in Section 3 it will be proposed that the notion of 'rule typology' applied to the syntax/lexicon dichotomy is one fruitful way of acquiring a realistic view of the interaction of the two components. Finally, Section 4 will have a brief survey of recent trends in the study of word formation in Japanese.

1. The syntax/lexicon dichotomy--The development of the Lexicalist Hypothesis

The basic unit is a word in the lexicon and a sentence in syntax. Words are usually memorized and used as such, whereas sentences are usually generated each time for the utterance. Noting this, Halle writes in his 'Prolegomena to Word Formation' (1973): 'There is a fundamental difference between the use of words and the use of sentences; one encounters new sentences but not new words all the time'. Thus it is a well-established view that the lexicon is basically a list of words with their idiosyncratic properties while syntax is a set of productive rules that combine them and generate sentences. The lexicon contains memorized knowledge while knowledge of syntax is productively used.

If it were the case that in natural languages words are not analyzable in any regular way, this simple view of the lexicon and syntax would be adequate for that aspect of grammar. In reality, however, the picture we get is far from that simple. Words are often made up of smaller units, free and bound morphemes, and words themselves combine to form complex words. The processes of word formation vary in character from quite irregular and idiosyncratic ones to mostly regular and productive ones. A problem then arises as to whether such word formation processes should be relegated to the lexicon or syntax. The basic unit, however complex it is, is still a word, although the processes somewhat resemble those of syntax in that they are productively used. To take an example from English, although there is no doubt that washable is a single word, it is part of an English speaker's knowledge that the suffix

-able attaches to a verb and forms an adjective with the meaning 'can be V-ed'. This piece of knowledge is productively used to form or understand a word of the form V-able.

As long as we maintain that there exist these two components, the lexicon and syntax, which seems to be a reasonable view, there are two basic approaches to take: one can either assign word formation processes to the syntactic component, even though they exhibit various degrees of idiosyncracy which still have to be somehow listed in the lexicon, or alternatively, one can assume that all word formation processes are part of the lexicon. The earliest work of relevance to this issue in the generative grammar literature is Robert B. Lees' The Grammar of English Nominalization (1960), which took the former approach. At that time any kind of regular relationship between two forms was to be expressed by syntactic transformations. This approach, often referred to as 'transformationalist hypothesis' has the advantage of keeping the lexicon only to idiosyncratic information while capturing all perceivable regularities by syntactic rules. Chomsky, in his 'Remarks on nominalization' (1972) questioned this approach. Based on some differences between derived nominals vs. gerundive nominals such as the morphological and semantic idiosyncracies and the surface NP structure of the former as opposed to the latter, he proposed that derived nominals should be derived in the lexicon. The insight behind his proposal, which is called the 'lexicalist hypothesis', is the idea that grammar consists of a set of interacting systems, and that the regularities we find should not be relegated solely to the transformations but should be distributed among different components. He called this task 'a demarcation problem' in the 1972 article; more recently, this idea figures more prominently in his work (e.g., Chomsky 1981) under the name 'modularity'.

It is important to note here that Chomsky (1972) proposed the 'lexicalist hypothesis' to deal with the derived nominals but not all derivational morphology. His proposals, however, have been extended and strengthened by a number of linguists in the development of 'lexicalism'. Jackendoff (1972, 1976) claims that all derivational morphology should be placed in the lexicon, where any morphological or semantic regularities between lexical items are captured by redundancy rules. Aronoff (1976) also claimed that all derivational morphology is in the domain of the lexicon. Recently, even inflection is claimed to be performed in the lexicon. (See Lieber 1980, Kiparsky 1982, Lapointe 1983, etc.). People subscribing to this view maintain the 'lexical integrity principle', whereby no morphological operation is allowed in the domain of syntax. Thus Chomsky's Lexicalist Hypothesis has yielded over the years some quite strong claims regarding the dichotomy between syntax and the lexicon.

2. Word Formation Rules

Once the word-level derivation was considered not to be part of syntax but of the lexicon, it was a natural move to capture the regularities of morphological derivation by some form of rules which are separate from syntactic rules. Jackendoff (1976) proposes morphological and semantic redundancy rules, and he maintains that creation is not the primary role of the lexicon, although he says that redundancy rules can be used in creating as well as understanding new words. It was Halle's 'Prolegomena to Word Formation' (1973) that "rediscovered" and brought back to light derivational morphology as productive rules in generative grammar.[1] His program for studies in word formation was followed by a number of linguists; Aronoff (1976), Siegel (1974), Allen (1978), Lieber (1980), Selkirk (1982) and so on. Through their work word formation is beginning to be considered to have much complexity and structure as a subcomponent of grammar. We will in this section discuss several basic issues concerning the overall properties of word formation rules and its role in grammar. Under each issue alternative views will be briefly surveyed and some problems with them will be pointed out. More specific claims concerning specific processes will be discussed in later chapters, after which we will evaluate how the data examined bear with those claims.

---

[1] See Lipka (1975) for relevant remarks.

2.1. Rule Formalisms

There have been basically three types of proposals as to what form word formation should take; lexical transformation, phrase structure rule, and no rule but only lexical insertion.

2.1.1. Lexical Transformation

In order to capture certain generalizations on verbal compounds in English, Roeper and Siegel (1978) proposed lexical transformation rules. They attribute the basic idea of introducing transformations in the lexicon to Vergnaud (1973). In their analysis a compound like coffee maker is derived by a transformation in the lexicon as follows.

(1) [make]V [coffee]N ---> [coffee maker]N

The first sister to the verb in its subcategorization is attached to the left of the verb at the same time -er is affixed. In a different paper(Keyser and Roeper 1983) it is claimed that this rule is an instance of the rule 'move-α' in the lexicon. It is also pointed out there that this rule operates on structural terms rather than on thematic roles. This is shown by the fact that nouns of various thematic roles can appear as the first element of the compound:[2]

(2) home-cooked (loc.), slave-built (agent),

   razor-sharpened (instr.)

---

[2] See Levi (1976) for detailed observations on the semantics of such compounds as well as a large collection of data.

What the first element of these compounds share is the fact that they would appear in a phrase following the verb (if we ignore the prepositions). This generalization, which is referred to as 'the first sister principle' by Roeper and Siegel, is structurally defined, and according to Wasow (1977), the rules whose domain is structurally rather than thematically defined are transformational rather than lexical. Note that Roeper and Siegel refer to the rule as a 'lexical transformation' in the sense that this is a transformational rule operating in the lexicon. We will discuss the apparently paradoxical status of this rule as so defined in the sections below. More details about verbal compounds will be taken up in Chapter II. It suffices to note here that transformation is one form of word formation rule that has been proposed for deriving verbal compounds because of the structural nature of the domain of this putative rule.

2.1.2. Phrase Structure Rules

Jackendoff (1976) notes that "the syntactic analogue of a morphological redundancy rule is a PSR and not a transformation." This idea has been most extensively pursued by Selkirk (1982). She defines WFRs as the X' version of context-free PSR, which she calls 'Word Structure Rules'. WSRs define the structure of a word in a tree form with the initial symbol X^0 (word), which may expand to symbols X^1 (stem), X^2 (root), and affixes. WSRs are intended to be generative devices for new words as well as redundancy rules for existing words.

The idea that WFRs and syntactic (i.e., sentence formation) rules are formally the same except for the difference in the levels of X' is an attractive one, but the question how far the parallelism goes has to be tested empirically. For instance, Selkirk's WSRs are based on the assumption that all word structures are headed, but it is far from clear in sentence structure that all the constituents are headed. It is also important to note that she claims (Selkirk 1982: 3) that although these WSRs are sufficient to characterize English word structure, it is only part of a typology of word structure systems of human languages. We can immediately think of a few processes of morphology which cannot be straightforwardly expressed with WSRs; namely, ∅-derivations, umlaut, reduplications, and dvandva constructions. Another problem with this system is the status of the category 'affix'. Although affixes are given a category status, this category does not belong to the X'-hierarchy with other categories according to Selkirk. Since affix is a major element in word formation, and some affixes are known to function semantically as adverbs (see Carlson and Roeper 1979), this lack of account of their status undermines the adoption of X' system and the putative parallelism between syntactic and word structure.

2.1.3. No WFRs

Lieber (1980) claims that there is no need for WFRs of affixation and compounding. Instead, she postulates lexical structures of an unlabeled tree form into which lexical items are inserted according to their subcategorization frame. The hierarchical structure (i.e., the category of the dominating node) is determined by percolation through which features of the head are copied onto the dominating node. This approach is supported by Kiparsky (1983), who gives the following points as advantages of lexical insertion approach over WFRs: (a) It unifies compounding and affixation; (b) Percolation is needed anyway for features triggering phonological processes; (c) It explains why affixation is never extrinsically ordered (see nation-al-iz-ation, organ-iz-ation-al) (d) It is in accordance with the fact that features that trigger WFRs are the features of the stem.

We have seen that the problem of appropriate rule formalism for word formation is quite open-ended. The important questions that remain are: what parallelisms there are between syntactic and word formation rules; what regularities should be represented in word formation rules. It is also important to note here that there hasn't been any rule formalism that can be claimed to handle all types of word formation across languages.

2.2. Level ordering and Adjacency Condition

One prominent claim of the recent studies of morphology is the so-called level-ordering hypothesis. This approach assumes that morphological processes are ordered according to the levels they belong to.

It was first proposed by Siegel (1974) that certain affixes (class 1) which affect the phonological form of the base morpheme and do not tend to have transparent semantics never occur outside those without such properties (class 2). This idea was adopted and extended by Allen, who added compound formation as class 3 processes. Allen (1978) also proposed the Adjacency Condition, under which WFR can affect only items in the adjacent morphological cycle, thus making WFR 'blind' to the internal structure or derivational history of the lexical items.

This development was recently taken up further by Kiparsky (1982, 1983), who calls his framework 'Lexical Morphology'. Kiparsky assumes that each level of morphological rules is accompanied by a set of phonological rules. The output of each level is a lexical item, and he postulates three distinctive levels for English. One noteworthy insight in his framework is the postulation that rules that are formally and semantically specific and idiosyncratic are ordered before rules that are more general and transparent, and a principle of Elsewhere Condition governs the application of these rules. He also adopts Allen's Adjacency Condition by using brackets to mark the output of each level and postulating the Bracket Erasure Convention, which erases all the internal brackets at the end of the level, thus making it impossible for the rules on a certain level to have access to the derivational history of a lexical item.

Although his framework makes a number of predictions which hold true for the English data, there seem to remain some problems. Most notably, there exist at least two types of violation of the level ordering he assumes, and he has to either allow some limited recursion of levels or block bracket erasure for such cases. One type of violation of the level ordering is exemplified by a word like analyzability, in which a level 2 affix able occurs inside a level 1 affix ity, and a word like ungrammaticality, in which a level 2 affix un has to attach to the stem before a level 1 affix ity does, in order to meet the subcategorization of the affix un(/__Adj.). These cases have led some people to separate morphological structure and semantic structure. (See Williams 1981, Lieber 1980, Selkirk 1982.) Further in this direction, Pesetsky (1983) proposes a mapping operation between lexical structure and Logical Form which takes the form of the 'move-α' transformation. Kiparsky (1983), on the other hand, proposes that the bracketing paradox of a word like ungrammaticality should be accounted for as an instance of morphological reanalysis.

The second type of level violation has to do with affixation to a compound or a phrase. It is exemplified by such words as <u>transformational grammarian</u>, <u>matter-of-factly</u>, <u>shirt-sleeved</u>, and so on. In view of such examples as these, Kiparsky says that a limited recursion from syntax to the lexicon must be allowed. One has to wonder, however, how 'limited' these exceptions could be when one considers the productive formation of adjectives like <u>shirt-sleeved</u>, <u>kimono-sleeved</u>, <u>long-sleeved</u>, <u>French-sleeved</u>, and so on, to take one example from English. Furthermore, there are a number of such instances of productive processes outside English found with polysynthetic languages or agglutinative languages. This point is crucial in evaluating the level-ordering approach to word formation. This will be a major topic of discussion in the following chapters.

Partly motivated by such counterevidence as discussed above, Aronoff and Sridhar (1983) recently proposed to abandon the level- ordering hypothesis and to adopt instead the classification 'word affix' and 'stem affix' without assuming any ordering between the two. 'Word affix' is defined as attaching to major lexical categories, while 'stem affix' attaches to morphemes. They claim that the facts claimed to follow from the level-ordering hypothesis can be accounted for by the different properties of these two types of affixes and the independently needed principle of Elsewhere Condition. They also claim that the bracketing paradox problems with level ordering disappear once they assume different structure for phonological word and morphological word, which they point out has been accepted above the level of word in the assignment of rhythm structure.

In spite of the problems, there seems to be an intuitive idea behind the level-ordered morphology, which is clearly articulated by Kiparsky's framework; namely, in the process of building words, phrases, and sentences, we find that the processes are more regular in form and meaning, as it is closer to the sentence level. On this end of the scale we have syntactic processes. Going in the opposite direction, we find the processes to become more and more irregular both in form and meaning, and finally, the forms (morphemes) are further unanalyzable and simply have to be listed; here we have the base of the lexicon. It therefore seems natural that, in dealing with word formation processes which lie somewhere in between, we perceive different levels of regularity. At the same time, it is also true, as people have pointed out in the past, that there exists some evidence against the strictness of such ordering of levels. We have to leave this issue open at this moment, but we should note one important question. That is, what implications do the predictions made by the level-ordering hypothesis and the problems with it have for the issue of syntax/lexicon dichotomy? This very question seems to have been neglected because the level-ordering hypothesis has been discussed with the assumption of the lexicalist position. We should, however, leave the lexicalist assumption in order to properly investigate this question, particularly in view of the following facts. The higher level word formation processes have very similar properties to phrase (i.e., syntactic) formation in terms of the regularity and compositionality. Further, some cases of bracketing paradox extend above the word level and involve phrases. And finally, if we are to recognize a phonological word to have different structure from a morphological word, as Aronoff and Sridhar (1983) suggest, the phonological word in their definition would include genuine cases of a phrase, even of non-constituents.

2.3. Head

'Head' is an important notion both in word formation and in syntax. The majority of words and phrases contain what can be considered as head. According to the basic definition, the head of X^n shares the features with X^n, X varying from a sub-word level to a phrasal level. In a number of frameworks with a version of the X' system (various works in GPSG, Lieber 1981, Selkirk 1982, etc.), a mechanism called 'feature percolation' is employed by which the feature of a particular element is transferred to the mother node. In word structure, the relevant features of each lexical item must be properly percolated to the dominating node, and become the features of the whole word, but it has not been completely agreed upon as to how that can be always carried out.

English compounds can be classified into two types depending on whether they are headed or not. With endocentric compounds in English, it is always the case that the rightmost element is the head. With exocentric compounds, such as [pick pocket]N, neither of the items is the head. There is another type of non-headed compound called 'dvandva compounds', which consist of the items of the same lexical category, where both of the compounded items can be thought of as head. This type of compound is not very common in English, but in some languages (see the discussion on Japanese in Kageyama 1982) it is a fairly productive process.

As for affixation processes, all the affixed items can be considered as headed, but designating the head is not a simple matter. It has been assumed by many that category-changing affixes are the head of the word. Since most suffixes are category-changing while only a couple of prefixes are (en-, be-) in English, there is a tendency that the rightmost element is the head; which is also observed with compounds. A problem arises when inflectional affixation comes into the picture. Clearly, the features carried by inflection such as number and tense have to be percolated to the mother node to become the features of the word itself, and yet the inflectional affixes do not determine the lexical category of the entire word. This fact has led to a discrepancy in the treatment of the inflectional affixes in terms of their headhood. Williams (1981) has treated them as head, while Selkirk (1982) is opposed to that approach. This problem actually bears on another important issue, which we turn to next, namely, whether inflectional affixes should be treated in the lexicon along with derivational affixes.

2.4. Inflection vs. Derivation

So far there seems to be no solid criteria established for distinguishing inflectional processes from derivational processes. (See Anderson 1982.) Nevertheless, it has been assumed that they are distinguishable for a majority of the cases, the difference being that inflection forms a paradigm of one lexical item, while derivation derives a new lexical item from an old one. Furthermore, inflection and derivation used to be considered to belong in different places of grammar. Even within the lexicalist approach the autonomy of word formation from syntax was claimed for derivational morphology and not for inflectional morphology. (See Chomsky 1972, Aronoff 1976.) More recently, it was proposed that inflectional morphology be treated in the same way as derivational morphology, extending the domain which the lexicalist hypothesis covers, while some people maintain inflection and derivation should be dealt with separately.

It has been noted by Lieber (1979) that the same morphological processes, umlaut for instance, often figure both in inflection and derivation, and certain derivational processes use the inflectional paradigm; for example, in German a verb-to-noun conversion sometimes uses the past participle stem of the verb such as Fund V,N. This finding has led Lieber to include inflection in the domain of the lexicon. This view is shared by Williams (1981), Selkirk (1982), and Lapointe (1983). Anderson (1982), on the other hand, takes inflection to be outside the lexicon. He defines inflection to be "what is relevant to syntax." He further says that "whether a certain category is inflectional or derivational depends on how much the category realized in inflection is integrated into syntactic principles," and notes that what counts as inflectional is a language specific matter. We should note here that the validity of Anderson's program depends on the clarity of the notion 'relevance to syntax'.

The controversy stems at least partially from the somewhat dual character of inflection; the process affects words in terms of morphology and phonology, but the interpretation and distribution of the inflected word is a syntactic matter. For instance, the nominative case may be realized by affixation, while lexical insertion of the NP into the subject position of a sentence must be performed on a syntactic tree. We will discuss a new approach below using the notion of rule typology, with which we will try to give an alternative to these existing analyses.

2.5. Semantics of Word

Since some words are structurally complex, the question naturally arises as to how form and meaning are related in them. More specifically, the question is, if certain regularities of word formation can be captured by assigning hierarchical structures, is the semantic structure isomorphic to the word structure?

This question became more prominent under the level ordering hypothesis. (See 2.2.) Coupled with the adjacency condition this approach does not allow a derived word to refer to the structure it had on a previous level, resulting in a strong prediction as to the way lexical items combine and can have semantic scope over each other, provided the semantic structure is isomorphic with the one assigned by levels. Allen (1978), in pursuing this restrictive approach, runs into a number of problems with the semantics. The most serious cases arise when the putative semantic structure involves prefixing or suffixing to compounds. Since in her scheme compounding belongs to level 3 while affixation belongs to level 1 or 2, compounds cannot undergo affixation as a whole, hence some problems arise. For example, the meaning of a verbal compound like _story teller_ depends crucially on the information that the second item is derived from a verb <u>tell</u> which subcategorizes a direct object such as <u>story</u>, but when the compounding takes place, ([story]N + [teller]N), that information cannot be available under the adjacency condition, since the affixation of <u>tell+-er</u> belongs to level 2. Allen was then forced to say that the semantic interpretation rule for verbal compounds (basically the same as Roeper and Siegel's First Sister Principle used as an interpretive device) does not obey level ordering. Put more plainly, she abandons the idea of having semantic structure isomorphic to lexical structure in word formation.

On the other hand, Allen approaches a similar problem with an adjective forming suffix <u>-ed</u> quite differently. One possible, and semantically straightforward, account of this suffix involves <u>-ed</u> attaching to X, X being a N (i.e., noun, compound noun, adjective + noun), yielding an adjective with the meaning 'having X, or bearing the characteristics of X', as exemplified by the following:

(3) [pencil point]-ed, [two leg(g)]-ed, [cold blood]-ed.

Such an account, however, cannot be allowed under the adjacency condition, which Allen maintains. She further claims that there is no justification for requiring X above to be even a semantic unit, not to mention a lexical one, since X is not always a compound but can be a phrase as well (see <u>two legs</u>, <u>cold blood</u> above), and suffixation to a phrase is "theoretically improbable" according to Allen.

The significance of this remark will be discussed later. Thus for these complex adjectives she cannot provide a convincing semantic account but can only give an insufficient one, namely, that 'cold blooded' has the semantic structure [cold]A + [blooded]A, with the second adjective modified by the first one, whatever that means.

Williams (1981) also points out several discrepancies between possible lexical structure and semantic structure, as exemplified by the following:

(4) [hydro electric]-ity, [Godel-number]-ing,
    [atomic scient]-ist

Williams tries to give some account by proposing a new notion of 'lexically related' whereby Y in the following tree can be related to X: (See Williams 1981 for details.)

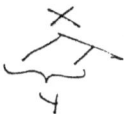

This notion of lexically-relatedness is, as Williams explicitly notes, clearly non-compositional. With this provision he maintains Allen's position that compounding cannot precede any affixation. It is noteworthy that even with this new notion of relatedness some exceptions do exist. The example Williams gives is 'reair-condition', with which there is no way one can relate 'air-condition' to the whole word; for this case he is forced to assume that 'air-condition' has been reanalyzed as a stem.

Selkirk (1982) agrees with Williams' claim that word structure is non-compositional, although she contends that compounding can precede level 2 affixation. This allows her to treat a case like set theoretic to have the structure [set]#[theoret+ic], with -ic as level 1 suffix. It also leads her to claim that when level 2 suffixes appear with a compound the structure can be ambiguous, as illustrated below:

(5) [bath room]-less / [bath] [room-less]

   [head strong]-ness / [head] [strong-ness]

It is claimed that both structures can be 'given the same interpretation, following the principle allowing for non-compositionality in the interpretation of word structure suggested by Williams'(Selkirk 1982: 111). This analysis seems absurd, for it allows for unnecessary alternative structures.   Once we allow compounding to precede some suffixation, a word like 'bathroomless' can be given a perfectly straightforward structure both derivationally and semantically, and there seems to be no case of a compound with the form [N] [N-less] with the semantic structure [N] [N-less]A. Also, the structure [head] [strongness] seems odd, as that structure would be realized as [head] [strength], with level 1 suffix on the adjective. Selkirk's analysis of these items demonstrates that once we allow non-compositional word structure, we can have a number of unmotivated structures assigned to words.

We have seen above in some detail that strict level ordering with the adjacency condition has led to the claim of non-compositionality of word structure semantics, which has a number of undesirable results. There exists an alternative approach in which the isomorphism between the semantic structure and the lexical structure is maintained, while the cases of mismatch are given separate accounts. This is the position Kiparsky (1982, 1983) takes in his framework of Lexical Morphology. We have already discussed in 2.2. how Kiparsky tries to account for the mismatch between lexical and semantic structures, which he calls the 'bracketing paradoxes', by proposing the following: first, allowing some limited recursion from a syntactic level back to word formation, in order to account for some instances of occurrence of a phrase in a word; second, postulating morphological reanalysis under certain conditions to accommodate level ordering violations. (See 2.2.) It was also mentioned that Pesetsky (1983), working under the same framework as Kiparsky's, recently proposed a mapping of lexical structure to logical form which involves a 'move-α' transformation, as an alternative to Kiparsky's proposal for morphological reanalysis. Although Pesetsky follows Williams and Selkirk in holding lexical structure and logical form to be not isomorphic, he departs from others by attempting to postulate a systematic mapping relationship between the two structures.

Of the two basic ways to treat the semantics of words discussed above the latter approach taken by Kiparsky seems to be more plausible and fruitful. By assuming the basic compositionality of word formation, we can narrow down the possible structures for each word, and even when there is a mismatch we can investigate exactly when and how (and perhaps under what circumstances) such a mismatch occurs, and postulate some principles or rules to account for them. Another important issue here is the fact that among the cases of a mismatch we have some that involve a unit that is larger than a word-- not only a compound but also a phrase. It is interesting to find out whether those cases are different in nature from word-internal cases. If so, that can be evidence for the strict dichotomy between the lexicon and syntax; if not, it can provide evidence against it.

3. Typology of rules

3.1. Earlier attempts for rule typology

So far we have been discussing various issues of word formation under the assumption that the domain of word formation is the word, and thus it is at least basically, if not completely, separate from syntax whose domain is those constituents that are larger than word. In this section we will discuss an approach whereby we look for the clustering of properties among various processes, lexical or syntactic, and see what the result can tell as about their status in grammar.

When Chomsky (1972) first proposed that derivation of certain nominals should belong to the lexicon and not to syntax, he listed a few properties of the process such as morphological idiosyncracies and semantic unpredictability. This was the first attempt made in generative grammar to classify rules of grammar according to some criteria. It was not until Wasow (1977), however, that more serious and detailed work was done on that attempt. What Wasow did was to try to give justification for having two types of rules separated in different components in grammar, namely, transformations in syntax and lexical redundancy rules in the lexicon, by postulating the properties that would distinguish them. The lexical rules are, according to Wasow, (1) structure preserving, (2) possibly category changing, (3) local in domain, (4) ordered before transformations, (5) with idiosyncratic exceptions.

3.2. Rule vs. operation: Dowty's (1979) proposal

Another important attempt of this type, this time between syntax/lexicon as well as between syntax/morphology, was made by Dowty. In trying to capture a realistic picture of the distinction between morphology and syntax, Dowty (1979) proposes that we separate the notions of 'rule' and 'operation'. He takes partial productivity and semantic unpredictability as the essential properties of lexical rules as opposed to syntactic rules, and claims that the lines between morphological operations and syntactic operations may not always coincide but sometimes cut across this distinction. He suggests that the operations might be constrained in some characteristic ways; for instance, morphological operations always give a fixed linear ordering of elements, while syntactic operations need not do so, or the product of morphological operations cannot be interrupted by syntactic operations. We will test these points and make some revision later. In any case, this approach of Dowty's is a remarkable breakthrough because we are no longer obliged to limit the domain of lexical rules to the word or to ignore the fact that some morphological processes share properties with syntactic processes. It also creates a potential for explaining facts observed in typologically varied languages as we will discuss later.

Table 1 shows this cross-classification of rules, taken from Dowty 1979, p.302, except for the symbols for each category.

(6) TABLE 1. TYPOLOGY OF RULES AND OPERATIONS

	Syntactic rules	Lexical rules
Syn. ope.	A. traditional syntactic rules (PS-like and transformation-like)	B. rules forming lexical units of more than one word, e.g., Eng. V-Prt combinations.
Mor. Ope.	C. inflectional morphology 'derivational' morphology when unrestricted and semantically regular (polysynthetic lang.)	D. rules introducing deriv. morphology, zero-derivation, and compounding, partially productive and less than predictable semantically

The classes A and D are what have been often assumed as syntactic rules and word formation rules respectively. B and C represent the new class of processes which have been a problem in the previous approaches. B consists of lexical units larger than a word which nonetheless are non-compositional in meaning (idioms, for instance) or are best regarded as a single 'word-like' constituent under certain syntactic rules (for instance, passivized complex verb: <u>taken</u> <u>advantage</u> <u>of</u>). The latter type of items have often been given an account as an instance of 'reanalysis'. (See Hornstein and Weinberg, 1980.) Class C consists of those word formations which are very similar to syntactic rules in their properties and have been claimed to belong to syntax by many people (see Sadock 1980 for such a case from West Greenlandic), or else have been simply unanalyzable for those who maintain the lexicalist hypothesis.

With this four-way distinction rather than previously held two-way one, Dowty has given classes of processes which could not previously be straightforwardly accounted for a proper place to belong to in grammar. We should note, however, that Dowty nevertheless maintains the basic lexicalist position that lexical rules are ordered before syntactic rules; thus, in the chart (6) above, rules of B and D always precede A and C, "since the domain of lexical rules is the set of basic expressions alone and does not include expressions derived by syntactic values, it is predicted that in any sentence in which both lexical and syntactic rules are in evidence, the lexical rules must have applied <u>before</u> any syntactic rules have been used, hence lexical rules are in a sense 'intrinsically ordered' before syntactic rules. . . . This theory turns out to predict semantic limits on what the interpretation rule of a lexical rule can do" (Dowty 1979: 306). We will see below, however, that it is not clear at all that this claim is true for English; in later chapters we will examine numerous cases of phrasal affixation from Japanese.

In the actual realization of the processes of types A to D in (6), Dowty notes that a single syntactic rule may involve both syntactic and morphological operations. He gives as one example the subject and predicate construction; the PSR (NP + VP) belongs to class A and the agreement on the verb, if the subject is a third person, belongs to class C. There is no problem of the ordering in this case, since A and C are both syntactic rules operating on the basic expressions.

3.3. Interaction of processes

What we will do in the rest of this section is to see how other combinations of processes are realized in forming an actual construction in English. By doing so we can find out the extent to which Dowty's program with the lexicalist assumption works and where it breaks down; more specifically, the question boils down to how and where the boundary between the lexical rules (B, D) and the syntactic rules (A, C) is relaxed in English. We will take up the possible combinations in turns.

3.3.1. A&B and C&D:
lexicalization

One interaction between processes belonging to A and B, and C and D is an unmarked one, by which what is producd lexically are fed to syntactic processes. So, on a word level a product of lexical word formation feeds syntactic word formation; for example, in the case of a compound noun with a plural suffix, a compound is formed in D and inflection is added in C. On a phrase level, a product of lexical unit formation is inserted to syntactic processes according to the category they belong to; for example, a verb-particle unit as a lexical unit of the V category is inserted accordingly to the syntactic structure.

The other interaction of A and B, and C and D is what is often called 'lexicalization', namely, what is produced syntatically can become unanalyzable as a unit on both word and phrase level. Let us look at the phrase level first. What is interesting about lexical unit formation is that it seems to always match some part of a surface syntactic sequence. Idioms generally have a structure of a phrase produced by phrase structure rules even though the meaning is non-compositional (cf. Zwicky 1978); as in _kick_ _the_ bucket (VP). Similarly, a number of lexical units are found to have a structure of PP or N', reanalyzed as an Adj: under-the-table (deal), over-the-counter (drugs), on-the-road (musicians), matter-of-fact (attitude), etc. Other lexical units do not necessarily form syntactic constituents, but through lexical unit formation are interpreted as a word-size constituent; for example, [take] [advantage of x] --> [take advantage of] x.

One interesting case of lexical unit formation seems to involve an output of syntactic movement. It is the formation of complex adjectives with 'tough' predicates discussed in Nanni (1980), as the following: an easy-to-sew pattern, an easy-to-take medicine. It is clear that the formation of these adjectives is based on the surface structure where the syntactic rule has applied: 'this pattern is easy (for x) to sew y.' The fact that this adjective can be formed from a rather complex structure where the surface sbject NP comes from a PP is shown by the following examples taken from advertisements.

(7) Here, the easy-to-feel-pretty-in bibbed cotton
    flannel dress in beige or black, S-M $315.
                                    (Vogue, Oct. 1983)

   If you've just remembered another hard-to-buy-for
   person on your Christmas list . . .
                                    (WFMT radio, Chicago)

The lexical rule of complex adjective formation as proposed by Nanni (1980) combines only an adjective and an infinitive form of a simple transitive verb, so it cannot generate (7).

It seems necessary that some kind of reference to the corresponding syntactic surface structure is necessary, from which a sequence of words are reanalyzed as a complex word.

Complex adjective formation is not actually strictly limited to easy-type adjectives as Nanni (1980) assumes, but seems to exist with other adjective constructions which have been considered to be derived by a rule of object complement deletion (cf. Lasnik and Fiengo 1974). See the following examples:[3]

(8) a. The girl is pretty to look at ∅
 --> a pretty-to-look-at girl

b. The soup is delicious to taste ∅
 --> a delicious-to-taste soup

c. The meal is ready to serve ∅
 --> a ready-to-serve meal

What these Adj.-to-V (part.) constructions have in common is that the subject NP (or the modified noun) corresponds to the deleted or moved direct object NP, and in that point they contrast with Equi-adjectives which cannot form a complex adjectives in the parallel way: *eager-to-succeed man, *ready-to-walk baby, *willing-to-talk person. This contrast seems to be related to the fact that the infinitives are subcategorized by the Equi-adjectives while they are more like modifiers with object deletion and

---

[3] The adjective construction with ready is not mentioned in Lasnik and Fiengo (1974). Although it belongs to a different semantic group from pretty -type subjective evaluation adjectives, ready seems to be close to them rather than to easy -type adjectives, since it cannot have a sentential subject: *It is ready to serve the meal.

easy-type adjectives. Further, it may be attributed to the difference in the nature of subject PRO of an infinitival complement. See Chapter II, Section 1 for the discussion on how this contrast may be related to the more general condition on word formation rules.

Thus we can say that the processes of lexical unit formation interact with syntax in two ways: one, a certain part of surface structure undergoes lexical unit formation; two, the formed lexical unit is inserted to a syntactic structure as a word-size constituent. As will be discussed in later sections, one important principle that governs such surface restructuring and reanalysis is the basic argument structure of predicates.

On the word level English does not have completely productive derivational processes except for a small class of such processes discussed below. With inflectional suffixation, we can also find only a small class of lexicalized items. One such case is a plural suffix which has been incorporated into the meaning of the word: *airs*, *arms*, *odds*, *pains*, etc. There are other plural forms which are semantically transparent but are morphologically irregular, which have been noted to occur inside a compound (cf. Kiparsky 1982): *teeth marks*, *lice-infected*. This can be a problem for Dowty's proposal, because an inflection formed by a rule of class C, which is supposed to apply after compound formation of D must break into the compound.

If we place the morphologically irregular inflection into class D, on the other hand, this problem does not arise. Similarly, the lexicalized plural suffix (i.e., semantically irregular one), can be grouped as D, and indeed they also occur in compounds: arms reduction, pains-taking, odds-making.

Another type of inflection that interacts with processes of D is the participle formation. For instance, derivation of adjectives from passive participle has been argued to be lexical (cf. Wasow 1977) as opposed to the syntactic verbal passivization. A few non-passive participles allow derivation of an adjective as well: fallen (tree), sunken (cheek), mistaken, etc.

In languages with more productive word formation processes this interaction of C and D is more active. It has been noted in Japanese that productive formation of passive and causative verbs are related to the transitivity paradigm through lexicalization of some forms (cf. Jacobson 1981, Miyagawa 1981, Kuroda 1982). This point will be taken up in Chapter IV.

3.3.2. B and D: apparent case of WF involving phrases

Some complex words in English which appear to be a product of word formation applied to a phrase actually are derived by word formation applied to a lexical unit. The following are such examples: un-[heard-of], un-[cared-for],

[laid-back]-ness (affixation); [hand-out]V->N, [sit-in]V->N
(conversion); [pick-up] truck (compounding).

Since these lexical units are product of lexical reanalysis on a sequence derivable by syntactic formation, it is natural that they give the appearance of word formation involving a phrase. On the other hand, their unproductivity separates them from a real case of phrasal suffixation and compounding. For instance, take the case of un-[V- part.]A as exemplified by unheard-of. Note that not every existing verb-particle combination can appear in this form but only those that can comfortably be used as an adjective in passive participle form can. Compare, for example, unheard-of and *unheard-about. In this sense this type of word formation should not be confused with those that involve rules of A and C discussed in the following.

3.3.3. A & D vs. A & C: WF involving phrases

Given the assumptions here, both the combinations of processes A & C and A & D involve phrase as a unit of word formation. The difference between the two would be that the processes of A & C have no lexical exceptions or semantic irregularities while those of A & D do. Actually, under Dowty's version of the lexicalist assumption that lexical rules must precede syntactic rules, the combination A & D by which a syntactically generated phrase enters a lexical word formation should not be possible; on the other hand, the combination A & C should be possible since A & C are both syntactic.

There are a small number of cases which can be viewed as belonging to one of the two combinations; it is unclear to me at this point how they should be distinguished. It may be that the combination of A & D is logically impossible, since a syntactic phrase is by nature productive and compositional (unless they undergo lexical unit formation), it is hard to imagine how a word formation rule that involves a phrase can be unproductive and non-compositional. I will assume here without much justification that any process of word formation involving a syntactic phrase is a combination of A & C.

What we are looking for, then, is a construction X + Y where one of X + Y is a freely generated phrase and the other a derivational affix. There seems to be a class of constructions in English that fits this description, illustrated by the following examples:

(9) warm-blooded, three-legged, tight-fisted, long-sleeved, deep-blue-eyed.

As mentioned in subsections 2.2. and 2.4., examples like these have been a problem for the strict lexicalist analysis of complex words. This word formation process is productive and compositional and can be schematized as: X+ed, where X is a N,' means 'having X or characterized by the presence of

---

'It seems that it is limited to a noun modified by one

X.' It therefore seems plausible to consider this formation as belonging to class C, often interacting with A to take in phrases as well (probably due to its productivity).

The class of verbal compounds of English exemplified below resemble this adjective formation in some respects.

(10) fast writer, hard worker, animal lover, party goer. three-time loser, early riser,

These words are quite productive and compositional, as the formation can be schematized as: X+er 'someone who is characterized by the act/state of V (X,V)', in contrast with so-called 'primary' compounds, whose meanings are lexicalized to various degrees.[5] Admitting these verbal compounds of (10) as product of syntactic word formation yields some interesting results.

As mentioned in 2.1.1, Roeper and Siegel (1978) proposed a lexical transformation to derive verbal compounds. According to Wasow's (1977) proposal to distinguish transformations and lexical rules, the term 'lexical transformation' itself is paradoxical. In fact, the formation of verbal compounds as we see it does not fit into Wasow's criteria--it is structure-dependent (as argued by Roeper and Siegel) in that the first element must be the first sister to the verb in its subcategorization frame,

---

word (or a compound as deep-blue) thus, *round (and) blue-eyed, *long blonde-haired.

[5] Of course, many verbal compounds do undergo lexicalization especially because of their noun category.

which makes it syntactic, while it is category-changing, which makes it lexical. On the other hand, in our classification of processes verbal compound formation seems to fit nicely as a syntactic word formation. It has both the word formation feature (i.e., category-changing by suffixation) and the syntactic rule feature that is due to the involvement of V'-phrase.

There are a couple of common peculiarities found with -ed Adjective formation and the verbal compound formation, which again separate them from primary compounds. Namely, they seem to exhibit some degree of transparency in that their subpart can be modified, inflected with comparative ending, and pronominalized by one, as shown below.

(11) a. John is warmer-hearted than Harry is.
b. This figure is exactly/more than five-cornered.
c. He is the earliest riser in the house.
d. I want to be a beautiful dancer, not a poor one.

Semantically they also seem to share the feature that they form a complex predicate as an adjective derived from a N' category or as a nominal derived from a V' category. (See Chapter II for more discussion of verbal compounds.)

In Japanese it is found that verb phrase is a very important category in various word formation processes. Chapter IV and Chapter V will be devoted to discussion of phrasal suffixation in Japanese, which presumably belong to this A & C combination.

3.3.4. B and C

The last combination of processes involves lexical unit formation and productive word formation. Since productive word formation are few in English, and they do not seem to feed lexical unit formation, the only notable interaction is the lexical unit undergoing productive word formation. We saw that lexical units undergo lexical word formation as a word-sized unit. Inflectional endings, which belong to syntactic word formation of class C, are found not to attach to them as a whole but only to the head word: cf. [tak<u>en</u> care of] (Passive), the [turn<u>ing</u> on] of the light (action nominal). So we may say that a lexical unit has dual characteristics with regard to the two types of morphological operations: it is transparent to inflection and opaque to lexical word formation.

3.3.5. Further remarks

Now that we have seen some examples of how the various processes are realized in English, let us elaborate a little on our observations. In the rule typology presented above, lexical unit formation (B) and syntactic word formation (C) are the deviation from more 'traditional' classes of A and D where the types of rules and operations match. Roughly speaking, lexical unit formation involves a 'reanalysis' of a part of surface syntactic sequence into a word, while syntactic word formation involves a kind of 'amalgam' of a phrase structure and a word structure. That is why lexical unit formation never 'creates' a structure,[6] while syntactic word formation is capable of creating a structure that does not match the phrase structure rules of the language. (See Chapter IV for such structure building and its consequence in Japanese.)

Formation of a lexical unit out of a group of words does not take place randomly. It seems that the examples of lexical units in English form either a transitive or an intransitive predicate. In an intriguing study on the subcategorization of complex verbs, Carlson and Roeper (1980) noted that rule-created complex verbs have what they call 'unmarked' subcategorization, namely, that of a transitive or an intransitive verb, rather than that of the more marked ditransitive verbs or verbs subcategorizing for PP. They found this generalization to hold across complex verbs of different origin; syntactic or lexical, phrasal or morphological.

On the other hand, there seems to be no reason for lexical units to be limited to those involving verbs. Wasow (1977) also questions the assumption that his lexical rules involve only verbs. We have seen that complex adjectives can also be a lexical unit. It is an open question at this point whether lexical unit formation is limited to

---

[6] Except for the case of a frozen syntactic phrase of an earlier stage, such as 'battle royal'.

argument-taking 'predicates'.

3.4. Cliticization

Although it is not often viewed as part of morphology or word formation, the process of cliticization is quite relevant to our discussion here, for it has some similar characteristics especially to the processes of class C in our classification, that is, syntactic rules with morphological operation.

Clitics can be described as 'unaccented words which must lean for support (the term 'clitic' originates from the Greek word for 'leaning') on a neighboring full word in their construction.' (Matthews 1974: 168) Among the well-known examples of clitics are Romance pronoun clitics ('je l'ai vu' Fr.), the English possessive marker ('the king of France's hat'), and the Latin conjunctive marker ('arma virumque'). As discussed in Zwicky (1977) in some detail, clitics can present a number of problems on various levels of linguistic analysis; syntactic, semantic, phonological, and morphological. Since it is beyond the scope of this section to discuss the full range of problems associated with cliticization, we will only touch on the aspects relevant to the framework of rule typology we pursue here. The basic problem that cliticization presents in our discussion is the following: although clitics often attach to a syntactic phrase, they are joined only to a part of that string. So, in the case of English possessive marker, for instance, although the marker applies to the whole NP, 'the king of France' in the example above, it attaches only to the last word. Thus if we were to strictly follow the phonological word boundary as marking the lexical unit, it would result in a mismatch between the semantic constituency and the syntactic constituency; a problem quite parallel to the 'bracketing paradox' of level-ordered morphology discussed in 2.2. above, except that this present case extends to a more significant boundary of syntax and the lexicon.

It is rather natural, then, that a number of linguists confronted with this problem of cliticization have proposed to treat cliticization separately from the rest of morphology and to place it so that the surface syntactic strings can feed cliticization, which is then viewed as part of phonological readjustment rules. Aronoff (1976) has suggested that cliticization should be grouped with inflection (which belongs to syntax in his view) as opposed to derivation. Zwicky (1982) and Zwicky and Pullum (1983), on the other hand, propose that cliticization makes a completely separate component from inflection or derivation, and maintain that cliticization component is ordered after the syntactic component. Zwicky and Pullum's Interface Model (see Zwicky 1982) predicts that separate components of inflectional morphology, syntax, and cliticization are all autonomous and do not overlap nor interact freely.

There is some evidence, however, that we cannot comfortably claim that cliticization is a postsyntactic phonological phenomena and dismiss it altogether from the discussion of morphology. After arguing that English n't is an inflectional affix as opposed to a clitic, Zwicky and Pullum (1983) suggest that it may very well have developed historically from a 'simple' clitic (a phonologically readjusted form of a free form). They also suggest that it could also look like a 'special' clitic (without free form counterpart), and that a special clitic and an inflectional affix can be very closely related. Thus although their contention is to separate clitics and inflection as discrete phenomena, the boundary cannot always be made clear-cut. This point is elaborated on by Sadock (1983a,b), who claims that on both ends of derivation and inflection there could be a gradual transition from cliticization to affixation. He takes data from English to show the inflection/clitic transition (cf. Sadock 1983a), and data from West Greenlandic to show the derivation/clitic transition (cf. Sadock 1983b). There is no space here to discuss his data, but instead we will briefly see the implication of the existence of such facts to our scheme of rule typology.

First, it is easy to see that the transition from clitics to inflectional affixes resides in the boundary between phrasal operation and morphological operation in syntactic rules (namely, A and C in the chart). In other words, although cliticization on the whole belongs to category c, the degree of 'wordhood' (i.e., how morphological the operation is) can vary diachronically or synchronically. Further, the more morphological the operation is, the more there is likelihood of clitics showing idiosyncracies and hence of the process become part of lexical rules (class D of our typology).[7] Sadock's (1983b) discussion of West Greenlandic noun incorporation suffixes is most revealing in this connection. He demonstrates that in West Greenlandic, a language with extremely well-developed morphology, various noun incorporation suffixes can be put on a scale according to their behaviors and properties, which shows there is a smooth transition from free-word-like suffixes to derivational bound morphemes. What this means in our rule typology scheme is that in a language where much syntax must be carried out with morphological operation, the unit of word must accommodate various degrees of lexicalization, and hence in such a case the boundary between C and D processes (syntax/lexicon boundary of morphological operation) must be particularly gradual. Note here that both inflection and derivation have been shown to exhibit fuzzy boundaries with phrasal operation processes; this observation is consistent with our contention that inflection and derivation are not

---

[7] Such idiosyncratic behaviors are part of what Zwicky and Pullum (1983) list as criteria for distinguishing affixes from clitics; namely, affixes are highly selective on hosts, their paradigm can have gaps, and they show phonological as well as semantic irregularities.

treated as two distinct components but are grouped together under the category of morphological operation, although we do not mean to ignore the difference that exists between them, especially that of relative ordering.

We have seen then that cliticization, which is basically a category C process, may not always be distinct from phrasal syntactic rules of A or from morphological lexical rules of D. There is a further problem that cliticization can present: if we assume that the cliticization processes (at least some of them) are phonological readjustment rules fed by surface syntactic structures, how can we distinguish the cases where a phrase as a unit undergoes some morphological operation (A and C combination discussed in 3.3.3.) from those in which a phrasal clitic is attached after syntax? We will take up this question in the later chapters when we discuss many potential cases of phrasal suffixation from Japanese as well as a few such cases from English. It will be argued that although we do need to attribute some of them to postsyntactic phonology, it is not plausible to treat all of them that way.

Some observations on language typology seem to be relevant here. Sapir (1921), in discussing morphological typology, suggests that the popular classificatory terms such as 'analytic', 'agglutinative', and 'polysynthetic' are not properly understood, but that we should view the notion 'agglutinative' as being in opposition to the notion 'fusional', thus referring to the mode of morphology, and the notion 'analytic' should be considered to be relative in degree to 'synthetic' and 'polysynthetic'. What seems to be relevant to the discussion of cliticization is the former opposition. Sapir says that 'agglutination' (or 'juxtaposition') as opposed to 'fusion' is characterized by directness and mechanicalness of affixation; in other words, low degree of idiosyncracy in phonology, morphology, and semantics. Note that this is part of the criteria used for distinguishing cliticization from affixation in relatively fusional languages such as English (analytic-fusional) and West Greenlandic (polysynthetic-fusional) as discussed above. It is therefore very important that we bear in mind this partial similarity between agglutination and cliticization when we look at an agglutinative language such as Japanese. In the later chapters when we discuss phrasal suffixation in Japanese we will have to look for the difference between processes that are clearly postsyntactic and those that interact with syntax. We will also consider how this partial parallelism between agglutination and cliticization affect the syntax/lexicon interaction.

4. Lexicalism in Japanese Syntax

Being an agglutinative language, Japanese exhibits rather complex morphology, especially in verbal suffixation: for instance, the following is an example of a verb with multiple suffixes:

(12) hatarak-ase-rare-ta-gari-sugi-ru.
    work-cause-pass-want-act-excessively-present
    'act excessively like (he) wants to be caused to work'

In the generative approach to Japanese syntax in the past, a number of verbal suffixes are analyzed as higher verbs taking a clausal complement (cf. Kuroda 1965, Kuno 1973, and Inoue 1976). In other words, for the purpose of syntactic derivations such as passive and causative transformations and case marking assignments, verbal suffixation is de-agglutinated and each suffix is treated as a higher verb. Recently, however, with the influence of the lexicalist approach and the autonomy thesis in general linguistic theory (which was discussed in Section 1), some attempts have been made to treat those verbal suffixes in the lexicon and to view the rules like passive and causative formation as lexical rules rather than syntactic transformations (cf. Farmer 1980, Miyagawa 1980). Under the lexicalist hypothesis it is significant that suffixes such as sase and rare are bound morphemes, since it follows then that they cannot be a unit in the syntactic operations. It is also emphasized that complex verbs V-sase and V-rare assign parallel sets of case markings to simple verbs. For instance, V(intr.)-sase assigns transitive case markings and V(tr.)-sase assigns ditransitive case markings. In sum, verbal suffixation is treated as a lexical rule that changes the argument structure and the case markings of the base verb. There has not been much rebuttal to the lexicalist approach to Japanese syntax from the 'transformationalist camp' except for Kuroda (1981a, 1981b), and this new approach seems to be gaining support. Kuroda (1981a,b) criticizes the lexicalist approach by pointing out that derivational morphology should not be given an independent theoretical status because syntax should be autonomous from morphology in the sense that the scope of a syntactic rule should not be limited by the unit in morphology, i.e., to a word. He attempts to illustrate this point by showing that the causative morpheme sase is a stem as well as a bound morpheme with the sentences where it appears independently; for instance:

(13) Taroo ga Jiroo ni utai mo sase-ta.
       NOM   DAT sing also cause-PAST
    'Taroo let Jiroo sing as well.'

The emphatic marker mo separates the main verb and the causative morpheme. Unfortunately, this argument is not so clear-cut, for there is evidence that suggests that this occurrence of sase is actually suru 'do' -(s)ase(which turns out to be s-ase); namely, in the parallel cases with the passive morpheme rare or the desiderative morpheme tai, the presence of suru is unambiguously required, as shown below.

(14) a. Taroo wa Jiroo ni utai mo s-are / *rare-ta.
       'Taroo was troubled also by Jiroo's singing.'

    b. Boku wa utai mo si-tai / *tai.
       'I want to sing as well (among other things).'

Kuroda (1981a, 112) himself notes this possibility that it is not conclusive as to whether <u>sase</u> is really a stem as well as a bound morpheme.[8] Nevertheless, the theoretical point Kuroda makes is a valid one: what belongs to syntax cannot be by assumption limited by the morphological unit. This point is especially important for an agglutinative language, where the morphological concatenation can be loose and transparent.

We will briefly elaborate here on this point just mentioned and discuss what seems to be problematic with the lexicalist approach to Japanese 'syntax'. One assumption to be questioned is that argument structure (or case frame) is uniquely associated with the word unit; i.e., complex verbs are assigned case frames that are realized in the syntactic structure while bound morphemes are not. As exemplified below, however, there are cases where periphrastic concatenation and agglutinative concatenation are not different in their function, and sometimes even in their regularity and transparency of application. First, take the productive causative formation and the periphrastic V-<u>te morau</u> construction.

(15) a. Taroo ga Jiroo ni uta o utaw-ase-ru.
        NOM   DATsongACCsing-cause-PRES
'Taroo causes Jiroo to sing a song.'

---

[8] In regard to this point, see Sugioka (1982) for the discussion on <u>suru</u>, which exhibits varying status from a bound morpheme to a free word depending on the environment.

b. Taroo ga Jiroo ni uta o utat-te mora-u.
      NOM   DATsongACC sing   receive
   'T. receives the favor of J.'s singing a song.'

In (15b) -te is a continuative marker on the verb and morau is a free word which can be used independently:

(16) Taroo ga Jiroo ni hon o morau.
     NOM   DAT bookACC receive
   'Taroo receives a book from Jiroo.'

Nevertheless, -te morau and -sase function in exactly the same way in the assignment of the argument structure and case markings to NP's, as well as exhibit the complete productivity. Further, although utatte morau consists of two words, they cannot be separated by an adverb, which, naturally, is the case with utaw-ase.

(17) *Taroo ga Jiroo ni uta o utatte kinoo morat-ta.
       NOM   DATsongACC sing yesterday receive-PAST
   'Taroo had Jiroo sing a song yesterday.'
   (cf. Taroo ga Jiroo ni hon o kinoo morat-ta.)

Should -te morau be treated also as a suffix to capture this parallelism? This move not only undermines the lexicalist assumption of separating phrase unit from word unit, but also would be problematic in view of the fact that the two endings do behave differently under the honorification process (which can be considered as a kind of inflection triggered by the feature on the subject NP), since this process applies basically to the head word of the verbal:[9] o-V ni naru.

---

[9]Although (18a,b) show a clear contrast, the honorification process of a complex verb is a complex matter, as discussed in Kuno (1983).

(18) a. Sensei ga Taroo ni uta o o-utaw-ase ni nat-ta.
       professorNOM DATsongACC sing-cause-HONOR-PAST
       'The professor made Taro sing a song.'

   b. Sensei ga Taroo ni uta o utat-te o-morai ni nat-ta.
      prof. NOM   DATsongACC sing receive-HONOR-PAST
      'The professor received T's favor of singing a song.'
      (cf. *o-utat-te morai ni nat-ta)

It is clear from the preceding discussion that the unit of word is less obscure under certain processes while clearly recognized in others. Our rule typology scheme captures this in the following way:

```
(19)      syntactic rules    |    lexical rules
-------------------------------|-----------------------------
 phrasal   V-te morau         |
-------------------------------|-----------------------------
morphol.   V-sase             |
```

The similarity and the difference between the two endings follow from the assumptions that the assignment of argument structure is a domain of the syntactic rules while honorification is an operation sensitive to the word boundary. Also the characterization above is consistent with the fact that V-<u>sase</u> can be lexicalized and incorporated into a compound much more frequently than V-<u>te morau</u>, because of its morphological nature.

Another such parallelism can be found with 'raising'-type constructions but with a more gradual transition from phrasal to suffixal. Note the following examples.[10]

---

[10] Examples of so-called 'raising' (20a,b) have been given much attention but their relationship to (20c,d) have not been discussed in the literature.

(20) a. Taroo ga [zinsei ga munasii] to omou.
        NOM   life NOM empty   COMP feel
   'Taroo feels that life is empty.'

  b. Taroo ga zinsei o munasii to omou.
      NOM life ACC empty COMP feel
   'Taroo considers life to be empty.'

  c. Taroo ga zinsei o munasiku omou.
      NOM   life ACC empty   feel
   'Taroo considers life empty.'

  d. Taroo ga zinsei o munasi-garu.
      NOM   life ACC empty-feel
   'Taroo considers life empty.'

Although (20a-d) are very close in what they express, they vary from completely bi-clausal (20a) to completely uni-clausal with the 'lower' predicate incorporated (20d); in between are uni-clausal case frame with retained complementizer (20b) and uni-clausal case frame with no complementizer (20c). We will leave the detailed discussion especially of the suffix _garu_ to Chapter III, but only note here that the transitive case frame of (20b-d) should not be given a completely separate accouont, in syntax (20b,c) on one hand and in the lexicon (20d) on the other. It should also be noted that there is no lexical idiosyncracy in the constructions like (20a) while in those like (20b,c) both the main verb and the 'lower' predicate are rather restricted, and in those like (20d) the adjective that can be suffixed by _garu_ are only those of emotional/physical feelings. (See Chapter III for the details.) It suffices to observe here that the lexical idiosyncracy does not clearly divide the word level (20d) and the phrasal level (20a-c), nor does the case frame.

We have provided evidence that the lexicalist assumption that the unit of word is uniquely associated with argument structure is too simplistic in the face of the actual data.[11] The other assumption that must be empirically tested is the claim that a bound affix attaches only to a word and not to a phrase. We have already discussed in Section 2 above some consequences of this claim in the general framework, and observed that for English it is mainly with inflectional morphology that this claim must be weakened. (For the discussion of a handful of such cases in derivational morphology of English see Chapter II, section 1.) For an agglutinative language like Japanese the situation is more interesting and we find many cases of derivational affixes attaching to syntactic phrases. We will devote a large part of the following chapters to the examination of such cases. They merit a careful study because although syntax and morphology do interact in a number of ways, there are properties particular to morphological operations (as opposed to the phrasal operations) or to syntactic rules (as opposed to the lexical rules) that constrain the possible types of interaction. As

---

[11] See Carlson and Roeper (1981) for the discussion of the parallelism between prefixed verbs and 'syntactically generated complex verbs' in English: e.g., unroll the rug vs. roll the rug out; mistreat him vs. treat him poorly.

a conclusion to this section, it is suggested that by departing from the simple lexicalist assumptions and by observing a broader range of processes belonging to derivational morphology (i.e., not just those that have been accounted for in syntax such as passive/causative formation), we will be able to approach closer to the true picture of how morphology and syntax interact in Japanese.

CHAPTER II

DEVERBAL NOMINALS AND COMPOUNDS

This chapter examines some aspects of verbal compounds in English and Japanese. What we will particularly be concerned about is the relationship between argument structure of a verb and verbal compounds. In Section 1 we will look at various frameworks that have been proposed to capture certain generalizations about this relationship and discuss the implication of those claims to our scheme of rule typology. Section 2 will examine Japanese verbal compounds with the focus on how abstract nominals are used in such compounds to reflect the argument structure of the source verb, and contrast them to the case of English verbal compounds. Section 3 will discuss some obervations on the phonological process 'rendaku' that frequently takes place in the compounds of Japanese.

1. English verbal compounds and argument structure

1.1. First Sister Principle

English verbal compounds, as opposed to primary (or root) compounds, can be defined with the following two points: they are marked by the morphological markings, -ing, -er, and -ed, and they have a verb base head (cf. Roeper and

Siegel 1978). The following are some examples of verbal compounds.

(1) truck driver, party goer, fast mover, good looker, house cleaning, eye catching, nice sounding, hand made, teacher trained, fresh baked, well written

Some generalizations about verbal compounds and the problems they present to certain frameworks of morphology have been mentioned in Chapter I. In this section we will discuss them in greater detail and propose an alternative approach to verbal compounds.

One salient generalization observed by Roeper and Siegel (1978) is expressed in their First Sister Principle (FSP): all verbal compounds are formed by incorporation of a word in first sister position of the verb. To exemplify how FSP works, we can look at the first example in (1) above. In truck driver, truck is a direct object and hence the first sister of drive. Contrast this with night driver, where drive has an intransitive meaning and therefore the adverbial phrase (at) night is the first sister. For the same reason, an unambiguously transitive verb cannot form a compound with an adverb: *quick-maker (cf. noise-maker). As mentioned in Chapter I (2.5) in the level-ordered approach to morphology proposed by Allen (1978) FSP cannot be a principle constraining word formation rules, since she postulates that compounding must be on a higher level than affixation, and her Adjacency Condition makes the rule of compounding 'blind' to the derivational history (that is, deverbal nature) of the compounded items. Allen thus proposes that FSP can operate as an interpretation rule, which is not subject to the Adjacency Condition. Allen is led to contend that verbal compounds and primary compounds are the same in formal nature, which claim is subsequently maintained by others (Selkirk 1982, Lieber 1983).

1.2. Verbal compounds vs. primary compounds

We will argue here that the analyses of English compounds which do not formally distinguish verbal compounds and primary compounds are inadequate and make a wrong factual prediction. First, let us recapitulate Roeper and Siegel's (1978) claim that verbal compounds are compositional and predictable in meaning, and extremely productive. Even though a number of verbal compounds undergo lexicalization, their basic meaning is always predictable. Thus <u>truck driver</u> differs from <u>bike rider</u> in carrying the meaning of it being a profession, but the basic meaning of both is "someone who V's X (professionally, habitually, etc.)" Following this pattern, one can immediately make a number of new compounds. Such transparency in meaning and productivity is typically syntactic, and sets verbal compounds apart from primary compounds.[1] For instance,

---

[1]This does not mean that the meaning of primary compounds is totally unpredictable. On the contrary, in a large number of cases their meaning can be systematically accounted for, and the reader is referred to Levi (1978) for a detailed study. Our contention, however, is that the meaning of verbal compounds can always be directly be

Downing (1977) discusses the result of the experiments she conducted in order to test the creation and interpretation of novel N + N (primary) compounds, and concludes that the constraints on them cannot be characterized in terms of the semantic or syntactic structures from which they are (conceivably) derived. Rather, she says, their interpretation is based on permanent non-predictable relationships of varying semantic types, and "their tendencies indicate more about the process of categorization than they do about derivational constraints on the compound processes." She further concludes it is the size of the temporal and spatial range of speech situations in which the compound is used to name an entity that constrains the speaker in his use of the compound.

Consequently, the analysis which does not distinguish the derivation of verbal compounds and primary compounds cannot capture this difference between them. The adherents of such an analysis, however, might argue back to this claim saying that incorporating FSP as an interpretation rule can capture the same generalization. For Allen, this was necessary to keep her scheme of level-ordered morphology, but it also led to the divorce of the semantic structure from the morphological structure. Selkirk (1982) claims that both verbal compounds and primary compounds are derived by the

---

obtained from their derivational processes, as opposed to primary compounds.

same set of WSR's, hence they are formally non-distinct. She gives what roughly amounts to FSP in the form of additional observations on the verbal compounds.[2] They are stated in terms of the functional argument structure of the verb (à la LFG). (a) The subject of a lexical item may not be satisfied in compound structure. (b) All non-subject arguments must be satisfied within that compound immediately dominating the head. Observation (a), which we will henceforth call "non-subject condition (on verbal compounds)" and discuss in greater detail later, is not particularly emphasized by Roeper and Siegel, since FSP is based on the subcategorization of the verb which (in Standard Theory at least) does not include subject. Observation (b), according to Selkirk, is a case of a more general principle holding on word structure as well as phrase structure; namely, all non-subject arguments of a lexical category X^i must be satisfied within the first-ordered projection of X^i. We will discuss the problems with this observation later, but it suffices here to observe that (a) and (b) together can eliminate the

---

[2] Selkirk actually gives a different definition from Roeper and Siegel's for verbal compounds; namely, she includes basically all deverbal nouns and adjectives (regardless of their endings) as an eligible head of the verbal compound, but she limits the non-head element to being a subcategorized (i.e., non-oblique) argument. See the discussion below that her definition fails to capture the salient class of compounds and that one of her observations on verbal compounds (as she defines them) does not hold true.

majority of the violations of FSP as far as Selkirk's own notion of verbal compounds (see fn. 2) is concerned. Note, however, that both (a) and (b) are merely observations on verbal compounds and they do not follow in any way from their derivational processes.

Let us take a brief look at another analysis of compounds where no distinction is made between verbal compounds and primary compounds. In Lieber's (1983) framework, all morphemes (stems and affixes) have lexical entries containing information about subcategorization, semantics, argument structure, and so on. They are inserted onto lexical structure trees according to their properties, and a set of feature percolation conventions ensure the proper features to be transmitted to the lexical head. She claims that we do not need to make any distinction between verbal compounds and primary compounds, but their possible occurrence can be predicted by Argument Linking Principle (ALP), which says that argument-taking words (V and P) must 'link' all internal arguments in the compound structure.³ The reader is referred to Lieber (1983) for the details of how this mechanism is supposed to predict possible and impossible compounds of English. We will only note here

---

³Lieber adopts Williams' (1981) notion of argument structure, where subject of the predication is called 'external argument' and the other subcategorized arguments are called 'internal argument'. By restricting ALP to internal arguments she automatically incorporates the 'no-subject condition.'

that even though ALP applies to those that involve argument-taking V or P, her compound structure always allows another structure where it does not apply; for instance, for truck driver:

(2) a.  b.

In (2a) ALP applies and gives the prediction similar to that of FSP (since the verb's internal argument is the direct object truck), but in (2b) ALP does not apply, so it is given an arbitrary interpretation (as a primary compound). It then seems that ALP does not really cover any more than FSP does, considering that it applies 'vacuously' to primary compounds; although Lieber claims it captures the generalization covering both types of compounds.

Now that we have reviewed three approaches where verbal compounds and primary compounds are not distinguished and the generalization of FSP is achieved by other means, let us go back to the question of whether their analyses can be claimed to be equivalent or superior to Roeper and Siegel's. We will argue here that they cannot. There is one factual prediction where these analyses go wrong; namely, the distribution of VP adverbs in the compound structure. Since a VP adverb can occur as first sister to a verb, it is allowed to enter a verbal compound in Roeper and Siegel's analysis (hard worker, fast mover, early riser, etc.). On the other hand, they cannot give an adequate account for the absence of -ly adverbs in nominal compounds, such as in beautiful(*ly) dancer. This problem can be solved by treating the adverbial marker ly as an inflectional affix which consequently never enters derivational morphology, as argued for in Sugioka and Lehr (1983). It can then be pointed out that a VP adverb may appear in verbal compounds but never in primary compounds; it is because VP adverbs enter a compound as a modifier to the verb from which a noun or an adjective is derived. For instance, the compound hard worker can be formed from [[work] [hard]]V' with hard as an adverb, but the primary compound [hard] [worker] cannot have hard as an adverb but only as an adjective, whatever interpretation it can have. It is then not surprising that in the approaches where verbal compounds and primary compounds are not distinguished the category adverb is mysteriously obscured. For instance, Selkirk does not have adverbs in her WSR even though she includes in her examples compounds with a non-ly adverb such as hard working. Similarly, although Lieber does not include adverb in the lexical categories that can enter compound structure, her examples include quick-considering, carefully-considering, etc. where the first element is labeled a Manner adverb.[4]

---

[4] It is argued in Sugioka and Lehr (1983) that all the apparent cases of ly-adverbs in a compound, such as carefully considering is an instance of a phrase, ADV + V-ing/ed, and not a compound.

This fact about the distribution of VP adverbs cannot be accounted for in an analysis where the deverbal source of the verbal compound head is not recognized.[5] It therefore supports the analysis which distinguishes verbal compounds from primary compounds by deriving the former from a verb and its argument.

1.3. An alternative analysis of verbal compounds

Having argued that the basic approach of Roeper and Siegel (1978) is correct, let us examine whether their analysis is actually flawless. There are a few criticisms which have been given by almost all of those papers mentioned above. One of the criticisms concerns the notion of 'subcategorization' as it appears in Roeper and Siegel (1978). They consider the subcategorization frame to appear as the following (R & S's (122)):

(3) Verb [DO] [Adv] [Inst] [Agent]

---

[5]There are problematic examples with S-adverbs: e.g., 'possible/ certain/accidental winner'. If they are derived from '(he will) possibly win', it suggests that the input constituent (V, X) can be a V' with a uniquely surface structure origin (presumably possibly is a sister to S in the base structure), which in turn suggests that the 'feedback' is from a surface syntactic structure to the word formation. However, this does not seem to be a genuine case of verbal compound, since FSP can be violated: e.g., possible winner of the Nobel Prize. This type of compounds remains a problem for all the accounts of compound formation including FSP and ALP.

In addition to those in (3) it is clear that they also need such arguments as [Locative] (home-cooked), [Goal] (church-goer), [Time] (night-driving), and so on. According to the commonly perceived view, however, subcategorization includes only those arguments that are obligatory with the verb, and not those optional elements such as time, manner, and so on. Selkirk, therefore, excludes optional arguments from her Functional Argument Structure and alters her definition of verbal compounds (cf. fn. 2). That does not seem to be the right move, however, since the generalization captured by FSP extends over adverbial arguments as well, as discussed at the beginning of this section with the example truck driver / night driver. In the case of Lieber (1983), although she also criticizes Roeper and Siegel for the complication on the subcategorization frame, and her ALP refers only to the internal arguments, it is also crucial to her account whether a certain item can be interpreted as a certain semantic argument or not. She excludes, for instance, ballad-picked as a possible compound, because the first element cannot be interpreted as a semantic (i.e., oblique) argument. It is clear that in order to capture a salient generalization about verbal compounds we need to include oblique argument of the verb as well. On the other hand, as far as the lexical rules are concerned, oblique arguments do not generally play a role.

Let us propose an alternative view: what we are dealing with here is not what is subcategorized by a verb but rather what can occur under a V'. Verbal compounds are derived from a possible expansion of V', V + X. If this V + X constitute a well-formed V', [X V]-er/-ing is a well-formed verbal compound. The case of passive participle is a little more tricky. Actually, the first element of a passive participle compound (ex. teacher-trained) is a first sister not to the main verb but to the passivized verb (trained (by a) teacher). It is not the affixation of -ed that form this complex adjective but rather a ∅-derivation. Let us list the verbal compound rules:

(4) a. [V X]V' + er ---> [X V-er] N

b. [V X]V' + ing ---> [X V-ing] N, A

c. [Vpass. X]V' + ∅ ---> [X Vpass.] A

Note that they turn out to be exactly parallel to nominalization and adjectivization of a simple V:

(5) a. V + er ---> N (ex. writer)

b. V + ing ---> N (ex. painting), A (ex. exciting)

c. Vpass. + ∅ ---> A (ex. surprised)

Another major criticism to Roeper and Siegel's analysis has been that they need to postulate a separate set of rules for deverbal nominals and adjectives besides the verbal compound formation rule, although they involve exactly the same set of affixes. In our alternative analysis, verbal compound formation can be perceived as an extension (in the sense it involves V') of nominalization and adjectivization of a verb, thus eliminating this redundancy.[6]

From semantic considerations it is easy to conceive how (4) and (5) are related. Take, for example, the agent nominal talker / song writer. A talker is a person who is characterized by the act of talking (a lot, usually); song writer is a person who is characterized by the act of writing songs (professionally, usually). Both talking and writing songs constitute an act, which is what is typically denoted by V', and after all, V is a possible expansion of V'. So we can say that nominalizaton and adjectivization in English with the suffixes -ing, -er, and -∅ can apply to V'. Note that these suffixes are the most productive and transparent among the various ways to nominalize and adjectivize verbs in English.

The claim that certain English nominalization and adjectivization processes apply to V' is not an uncontroversial one. On the contrary, it violates the fundamental assumption of the lexicalist approach that no phrasal category can enter word formation. This position is maintained in all of above-mentioned studies on verbal compounds. This is one of the reasons why the simple

---

[6]Kiparsky (1983), who basically supports Roeper and Siegel's analysis also collapses what in his formulation of rules correspond to (4a,b) and (5a,b) (not the ∅-derivation of adjectives). However, in his lexicalist framework, he does not consider V' to enter his rules. He consequently has the same problem as the others in defining what X can be in [X V].

generalization that a well-formed V' (V X) can derive a verbal compound had to be captured in other ways, as discussed above. In Chapter I we have already touched on the consequence of allowing a phrasal category in word formation . In our rule typology scheme the verbal compound formation involves the interaction of A and C, and as mentioned there, that seems to give the correct characterization of the process. Namely, in the analysis by Roeper and Siegel verbal compound formation seemed to have a dual characteristic of being syntactic (structure dependency in its condition) and of being lexical (category-changing) according to Wasow's (1977) criteria. By viewing it as a process of A and C interaction in our typology, we can say that the syntactic nature of the process lies in its phrasal input (A) and the lexical nature of the process lies in its being a morphological derivation (C). Indeed, the productivity and the semantic compositionality of verbal compound formation are attributed not only to these particular suffixation processes but also to the phrasal expansion under V'. Note also that our rules in (4) are simple derivational rules and do not involve the mechanism of transformation. We will explain below that a morphological well-formedness condition restricts the form of the output (e.g., number and order of elements).

As mentioned earlier (Chapter I: 3.3.3.) there exists in English a class of complex adjectives which has similar

properties to the verbal compounds, as exemplified by
warm-hearted, three-legged, and so on. We have already
discussed the type of problems these compounds have given
for the framework of level-ordering morphology (cf. Chapter
I: 2.5.). Clearly, we can give a straightforward analysis
to this class of compounds in a similar way to the
derivation of verbal compounds.

(6) N'(X N) + ed ---> [[X] [N-ed]] A

As in the case of verbal compounds, N' can also be a simple
N (ex. wing-ed), and in all cases the basic compositional
meaning is: characterized by the possession or the presence
of N'.

Bresnan (1982a) gives a nice piece of evidence showing
that the input N' in (6) must be a syntactically well-formed
N'. An adjective which cannot appear in the prenominal
position (ex. my foot is asleep / *asleep foot) also cannot
appear in the compound in question: *asleep-footed. From
this fact Bresnan suggests that "syntactic adjacency may be
a general condition on the morphological incorporation of
independent lexical categories into single words," but then
she concludes that "it is unlikely that this 'global'
condition is a formal condition of grammar, but rather must
be a factor that affects perception and lexicalization." We
cannot accept these remarks on the following grounds.
First, syntactic adjacency is not a general condition of the
process of this type, as evidenced by verbal compound

formation; in the case of verbal compounds, the order of elements under V' must be reversed to fit the formal constraint of compounds (see below). Secondly, this complex adjective formation is fundamentally different from lexicalization of a phrase (i.e., lexical unit formation belonging to C in our typology) in that what is involved is a compositional and productive phrase. Consequently, we regard this example supplied by Bresnan as supporting evidence for our rule (6).

The similarity between the verbal compounds and these complex adjectives in terms of their transparency was also pointed out in Chapter I (cf. (11)). The fact that they can internally take a comparative or superlative ending (ex. warmer-hearted, earliest riser), for instance, supports our proposal that these forms are derived by syntactic processes as opposed to the primary compounds. We consider comparative affixation as inflectional (class C) and, thus, often interact with phrasal operations.[7] The examples above have the comparative marker on X' level before the affixation takes place; [warmer heart] N', [rise earliest] V'. For the complex adjectives, there naturally is another slot for the comparative marker, with its domain being the entire compound: <u>more</u> <u>warm-hearted</u>.

---

[7]This applies also to the periphrastic markers <u>more</u>, <u>most</u>, with which the comparative endings alternate.

We have thus recognized three types of suffixation processes that can apply to V' and one that can apply to N'. Although such a claim cannot be consistent with a strict lexicalist position, postulating them does by no means allow unrestricted interaction between syntax and the lexicon. As observed in the discussion of our rule typology scheme, morphological operations typically exhibit lexical properties, and in many languages (such as English) the interaction between A (syntactic-phrasal) and C (syntactic-morphological) is quite limited. Among all the derivational processes in English, these four suffixation processes we postulated here seem to mark the exception. Further, even though they include V' and N' category, there seem to be some formal constraints on the output word, making them parallel in form to the ordinary compounds in English. First, they must be right-headed, and hence the affix must attach to the head V and the head N. As a consequence, the order of elements in a verbal compound is the opposite (X V) from that in V' (V X). Secondly the compound cannot consist of more than two words; drive truck (at) night / * night truck driver.[8] In complex adjectives, the modifier to the head N must be a single word (or a compound): deep-blue eyed / * round (and) blue eyed.

---

[8]On the other hand, since compound formation is recursive, compounds themselves can be compounded with other words; cf. [coffee maker] [maker]. If this example above is interpretable, it is structured: [night] [truck driver].

1.4. No subject condition

It has been mentioned that people have observed what can be called a 'no subject condition' on verbal compounds: in a verbal compound the first element cannot bear the subject relation to the verb. It was pointed out earlier that Selkirk (1982) had to state this condition as a separate observation because her observations on verbal compounds are based on their functional argument structure. Lieber (1983) achieved a parallel effect by restricting the argument linking to internal arguments. But for neither of them is this condition a natural consequence of the compound formation. In our analysis this condition follows directly from the rule because V' cannot include the subject. This point is significant in that this condition seems to be absolutely exceptionless for the verbal compounds, and therefore it distinguishes verbal compounds from primary compounds with similar meanings, as shown in the following.[9]

(7) a. *heart failing / heart failure
b. *population growing / population growth
c. *rain falling / rainfall
d. *earth quaking / earthquake

Note that Selkirk's notion of verbal compounds includes all the items in (7), for which her observation of 'no subject condition' does not uniformally hold. Similarly, although

---

[9]Note that only -ing nominals have the potential of incorporating the subject. In agent nominals the subject relation is expressed(?) by the suffix, and in passive compounds the subject relation is always outside the compound (typically the element modified by the compound): hand-made objects.

Kiparsky (1983) captures the contrast of (7a,b) by his rules, the contrast in (7c,d) is not explained (as he admits), for he includes ∅-formation verbs in verbal compounds.

From semantic considerations, it can be pointed out that a verbal compound of the form V'-ing usually denotes a generic name for an act, since that is what V' generally denotes. On the other hand, what a subject NP and a verb denote is not an act, but is an event. It consequently seems natural that even with primary compounds this relation is not commonly realized (i.e., named), and many of such examples seem to refer to some sort of natural phenomena, as exemplified in (7) above. This tendency is also attested with Japanese compounds of the similar kind. (See section 2.) Nevertheless, the fact that verbal compounds cannot express such cases is significant and supports our analysis based on V'.

1.5. The generic condition on the realization of the argument structure

We will now examine one interesting condition regarding how the argument structure of a verb is realized both lexically and syntactically. Selkirk's (1982) above-mentioned observation (b) about verbal compounds states that all non-subject arguments must be realized in compound structure. This generalization is similar in spirit to Lieber's (1983) ALP, which states that all internal arguments must be linked in compound structure, although it applies in a very different framework. Selkirk (1982: fn.15) admits the inadequacy of her generalization in the face of the examples supplied by Roeper, which involves the agent argument appearing outside the compound: cigarette-smoking by children. It seems possible, however, to handle this example by saying that agent arguments can appear outside the compound since they typically bear the subject relation to the verb and hence cannot enter the compound structure except for the case of passive compounds such as teacher-trained. Note that even with passive compounds it is possible for the agent argument to appear outside: hand-made by children.

One interesting fact we can observe about this realization of the agent argument with a by-phrase is the following contrast:

(8) a. Cigarette-smoking by children is upsetting.
b. ?Cigarette-smoking by some students upset me.
c. *Cigarette-smoking by my son upset me.
d. *Cigarette-smoking by John upset me.

(9) a. Church-going by young people is on the decline.
b. *Church-going by John pleases his mother.

It seems that the agent phrase appearing with a verbal compound is largely restricted to generics. It turns out, on the other hand, that the genitive realization of the agent is not restricted in the same way:

(10) a. John's cigarette-smoking upset Mary.
b. John's church-going pleases his mother.

It seems that this is due to the fact that the genitive marker can express a wide range of relations, and in this case it seems to express something like 'John's habit of V'-ing.'

It has long been noted (Postal 1969 and others) that nouns in a compound cannot be referential. For instance, they cannot be an antecedent to an anaphora:

(11) *John is a horse thief, but at least he fed it/them.

Similarly, Levi (1978) points out that a <u>woman-hating</u> <u>editor</u> "could only describe an editor who hated women in general, but not (atypically) one particular woman." It seems then that what can be called a 'generic condition' for compounds extends to the syntactically realized agent argument of the compound as well. It is unclear to me at this point what consequences this observation has for the general question of how the syntactic realization should be related to compound formation. Nevertheless, the generic condition seems to be a salient generalization, and we find below that it extends to some other cases as well.[10]

There are a couple of fairly productive ways to adjectivize verbs, namely the suffixation of <u>-able</u>, and the un-passive formation. We can observe that the generic

---

[10] Roeper (1984, ms) discusses the syntactic and lexical realizations of thematic roles in GB framework. He talks about the appearance of the agent phrases with various deverbal constructions, but does not consider any particular constraints on them. His examples, however, gave me some hints for the observation made here.

condition seems to be applying to them as well, as exemplified below:

(12) a. This game is playable by four people.
b. *This game is playable by John.

(13) a. This problem is solvable by a ten-year-old.
b. *This problem is solvable by John.
(cf. This ploblem can be solved by John.)

(14) a. This phenomenon was undescribed by scientists.
b. ?*This phenomenon was undescribed by Chomsky.
(cf. This phenomenon was not described by Chomsky.)

The existence of such a generic constraint seems to follow from the nature of these derivational processes. Verbal compounds, as mentioned before, express generic names of acts (as opposed to specific instances of them), and -able or un-passive adjectives express general properties (as opposed to specific states), and thus they are not semantically congruous with a specific or a referential agent. The generic nature of these derivational processes stands in contrast with the more syntactic and periphrastic means of expression: verbal compounds vs. gerunds, un-passive vs. not + passive, -able vs. can be V-ed.

We find another instance where the generic condition may be considered relevant in the lexical unit formation of complex adjectives discussed in Chapter I (3.3.1), although they are not related to the processes discussed in this section. We observed that easy-type adjectives and object complement deletion adjectives can form a complex adjective with their infinitival complements: easy-to-please, pretty-to-look-at, ready-to-serve. On the other hand, it was noted that equi-adjectives cannot form complex adjectives in the same way: *eager-to-succeed, *ready-to-walk, *willing-to-talk. Among other things one salient difference between these two classes of adjectives is the nature of the subject PRO of their infinitival complement. Namely, the former class of adjectives have PRO of arbitrary reference, while the equi-adjectives have subject-controlled PRO:

(16) a. John is easy [PROarb to please t]

b. Johni is eager [PROi to succeed]

If we can assume that PROarb correspond to a generic NP and a controlled PRO to a referential NP, we can explain the facts here as another instance of the generic condition.

2. Deverbal nominals and compounds in Japanese

The basic nominal form of a verb is the same as the infinitive form (renyoo-kei) in Japanese: verb root + i, or when the root ends with e, i, no overt suffix is added. This form participates in various productive compound formations as a nominal as well as in syntactic environment as an infinitive. As we will see below, the homophony of these two forms result in cases where it is hard to determine whether a certain occurrence of this form is a nominal or an infinitive. The following list shows the basic types of derivations in which this form of a verb appears.[11]

(17) simple nominalization: VN (deverbal nominal)

    a. asob-u --> asob-i 'play'
    b. (applies to a complex verb form of V-inf. + V)
       uke-ire-ru (receive-take in) --> uke-ire 'acceptance'

(18) compounding of VN's: [VN VN]

    a. kiri-uri (cut-sell) 'selling by pieces'
       (cf. hakari-uri (weigh-sell) 'selling by the weight'
    b. awate-gai (hurry-buy) 'hasty purchase'
    c. hasiri-gaki (run-write) 'scribble'

(19) dvandva compounds of VN's

    a. uri-kai (sell-buy) 'selling and buying, trade'
    b. yuki-ki (go-come) 'going and coming, traffic'

(20) [X VN] compounds

    a. [N VN] yuki-doke (snow-melt) 'thawing of the snow'
    b. [N VN] kutu-migaki (shoe-polish) 'shoe polish(er)'
    c. [ADV VN] haya-oki (early-rise) 'early rising/riser'

(21) [VN X] compounds

    a. hosi-gusa (dry-grass) 'hay'
    b. kai-mono (buy-thing) 'shopping'

(22) reduplication

    a. [VN VN]A tiri-ziri (scatter) 'all scattered'
    b. [V-inf. V-inf.]ADV kaki-kaki 'while writing'

(23) suffixation

    a. (adjectival) aruki-tai (walk-want) 'want to walk'
    b. (nominal) aruki-kata (walk-way) 'way of walking'

---

[11] There is a phonological process called 'rendaku' (literally 'sequential voicing'), which changes the voicing of the initial voiceless consonant of the second element under certain conditions. In (18b), for instance, kai is changed to gai in the compound structure. For some observations on this process in relation to compound formation, see Section 3.

In what follows we will first consider the properties of deverbal nominal compounds (20)-(21) in Section 2.1. In Section 2.2. we will look at nominal suffixation (23) and some related constructions.

2.1. Deverbal compounds

2.1.1. Types of deverbal compounds

Compound formation has been given some attention by the generative grammarians working on Japanese. Okutu (1975) sketches a transformational analysis in which each compound has a sentential source. Makino (1976) argues against a syntactic approach to compounds because of the large amount of semantic idiosyncracy involved in compounds. The topic is taken up again recently in Kageyama (1981), where he also argues against transformational derivation. Among other things, he points out that the verbal compounds (which he calls 'nominalization compounds') in Japanese have a much wider range of meaning than their English counterparts with -ing, and also that the grammatical relations of the 'incorporated noun' can be much more varied. As an illustration, let us look at the possible range of [X VN] compounds, classifying them by the meaning of the compound and the function of the first element:

(24) types of [X VN] compounds (+: examples from Kageyama 1981)
A. Agent
  a. DO: mono-tori (thing-rob) 'thief'
      kane-moti (money-own) 'wealthy person'

B. Instrument
  a. DO: nezi-mawasi⁺ (screw-turn) 'screw driver'
     kan-kiri⁺ (can-cut) 'can opener'

C. Result/Product
  a. DO: yasai-itame (vegetable-fry)⁺ 'fried vegetable'
  b. SU (Vt): musi-kui (bug-eat) 'a hole in cloth, etc. caused by a bug eating it.'
  c. SU (Vi): mizu-tamari⁺ (water-accumulate) 'puddle'
  d. by-Agent: musi-sasare (bug-be stung) 'bug-sting'
  e. Instrument: kami-zutumi (paper-wrap) 'something wrapped with paper'

D. Place/time
  a. DO: mono-hosi (thing-dry) 'a veranda for hanging laundry'
  b. SU (Vi): hi-gure⁺ (sun-set) 'sunset (time)'

E. Act(-suru)/ Event(-ni naru,'become' -ga aru'there is-'
  a. DO: kane-mooke (money-profit) 'making profit'
  b. SU (Vi): yama-kuzure (mountain-collapse) 'avalanche'
  c. SU (Vt): kami-kakusi (god-hide) 'mysterious dissapearance'
  d. IO: hito-makase⁺ (person-depend on) 'being dependent'
  e. Goal: tera-mairi (temple-visit) 'temple-going'
  f. Source: ie-de (house-leave) 'running away from home'
  g. Instrument: suna-asobi⁺ (sand-play) 'playing with sand'
  h. Time: yo-asobi⁺ (night-play) 'go out and have fun at night'
  i. Adverb: waka-zini⁺ (young-die) 'early death'
  j. 'like a N': kaeru-tobi (frog-jump) 'jump like a frog'

F. Nominal predicate (-da 'be X')
  a. DO: oya-nakase (parent-cause to cry) 'being a bad child'
  b. Goal: gaikoku-yuki ⁺(foreign land-go) 'foreign bound'
  c. Source: huransu-gaeri (France-return) 'returnee from F.'
  d. Time: Meiji-umare ⁺(Meiji era-born) 'Meiji generation'
  e. Place: Osaka-sodati (Osaka-grow up) 'have grown up in O.'

Although this is not an exhaustive list, one can see the vast range of meanings expressed by the [X VN] compounds. When we consider the fact that they are formally non-distinct from each other, it is not surprising that some of them can be ambiguous depending on the context of use: for instance, <u>kutu-migaki</u> (shoe-polish) can be Agent 'shoe polisher', Instrument 'shoe polish' or Act 'shoe polishing'. Note that the English counterparts are marked with different suffixes according to their meanings.[12]

Compared with [X VN] compounds, [VN X] compounds show less variation. They can be classified in two categories: Act nominal and modified nominal.

(25) types of [VN X] compounds
A. Act nominal
   DO: wasure-mono (forget-thing) 'forget/leave something'
       oki-tegami (leave-letter) 'leaving a letter (for someone to read)'
       yaki-mono (bake-thing) 'pottery'

B. Modified nominal (N that (is) V-ed)
   hosi-gusa (dry-grass) 'hay'
   yaki-zakana (bake-fish) 'broiled fish'
   nokori-yuki (remain-snow) 'remaining snow'
   asobi-ba (play-place) 'playing ground'
   kiraware-mono (be disliked-person) 'unpopular person'

Although (25A) and (25B) are formally similar, only the former can be used in the frame 'VN-o suru', and the latter are all concrete nouns. For both of them, only N can be the second element, unlike [X VN] compounds.

2.1.2. Analysis for the deverbal compounds

We can observe from (24) and (25) that the Japanese compounds involving deverbal nominals cannot be given a simple analysis parallel to what we gave for English deverbal compounds. It was claimed in Section 1 above that English deverbal compounds are derived by suffixation to V',

---

[12]English nominalizing suffixes do carry multiple meanings: ex. -er: Agent/Inst., -ing: Act/Product, etc. Nevertheless, compared with the Japanese cases, they contribute in distinguishing the possible meaning of the deverbal compound. See below for more discussion on the function of suffixes.

and that FSP restricts items that can form a deverbal compound. Japanese compounds in (24) and (25), on the other hand, do not appear to have such restrictions. We can spot a number of cases which would violate FSP: the non-deverbal element can be subject of both transitive and intransitive verbs (24E.b,c), Indirect object (24E.d), Instrument of a transitive verb (24C.e), and so on. The issue of whether Japanese has a V', and if it does, on what level, is a controversial one, but given such diversity of data here, it is clear that one cannot restrict the items in the compounds using such notions as V' or FSP.

This is not to say that there is no pattern at all in the way these compounds are formed. Actually, transitive verbs and DO are the most frequent combinations, and among the different types Agent nominals (24A), Instrument nominals (24B), and [VN-N] Act nominals (25A) seem to allow only DO as the non-deverbal element. There is also a certain amount of correlation between the type of relationship V and X hold and the way the compound is used. For instance, a rather unlikely type of compound [SU, Vt] cannot be used as an ordinary action nominal but rather is used in a passive-like context with the direct object of the verb as the subject of the sentence:

   (26) a. Kodomo ga kami-kakusi ni at-ta.
          child NOM god-hide   DAT encounter-PAST
          'A child disappeared (as if taken by God).'

      b. Kare wa hito-zuki ga suru.
         he TOP person-like NOM do
         'He is likable.'

    c. Kare wa hito-warai ni na-tta.
       he TOP person-laugh at DAT become-PAST
       'He became a laughing stock.'

It is also interesting that the cases of [SU Vi] seem to be limited to some types of natural phenomenon:

(27) ame-huri (rain-fall) 'rainfall'
     zi-suberi (land-slide) 'landslide'
     kaza-muki (wind-turn) 'the direction of the wind'
     hi-deri (sun-scorch) 'drought'

These compounds correspond to the English compounds with ∅-suffix that was discussed in relation to the 'no-SU conditon' in Section 1, such as sunset, landslide, snowfall, and so on.[13]

We are not going to discuss the semantics of each type of compound, but this brief discussion of some of them leads us to think that it is the lack of a suffix to indicate the semantic category of the compounds (unlike the case of English deverbal compounds) that seems to allow various usages and hence the wide range of the relationships between V and X. This lack of suffix also is responsible for the mismatch between the category of the morphological head element and the compound itself. In regard to this point, Kageyama (1982), after stating that the compounds should be derived in the lexicon, assumes that a lexical reanalysis of the following sort often takes place.

---

[13]Mikami (1953) makes the remark that the subject NP and a passivizable verb ('noo-doosi' Vt and some Vi's) cannot form a compound, and only non-passivizable verbs ('sho-doosi' some Vi's) can form a compound with the subject NP.

(28) a. [kane-moti] VN-->N (money-own) 'wealthy person'
     b. [kai-mono] N-->VN (buy-thing) 'shopping'

Although this account can adjust the frequent mismatch in categories, it allows arbitrary switching between N and VN, which is not plausible in view of the observations below.

Looking again at examples of various compounds in (24) and (25), we see that the cases where this mismatch does not occur are [X VN] action nominals (24E) that can be used as VN (-o suru), and [VN N] modified nominals (25B) that are used as N. Now, except for those that have rather idiosyncratic usages (as exemplified above), the rest of [X VN] compounds can be straightforwardly seen as having an understood ∅-head.[14]

(29) A. Agent: kane-moti-∅ (money-own) 'wealthy person'
     B. Inst.: tume-kiri-∅ (nail-cut) 'nail-clipper'
     C. Result: musi-kui-∅ (bug-eat) 'a hole made by bugs'
     D. Place: mono-hosi-∅ (thing-dry) 'a veranda for drying laundry'
     E. Time: hi-gure-∅ (sun-set) 'sunset time'
     F. Act: ie-de-∅ (home-leave) 'running away from home'

In fact the transformations proposed by Okutsu (1975) and Makino (1976) (although the latter eventually rejected that approach) derive these compounds from a relative clause structure with an abstract head: i.e., [kane o motu] hito 'a person who has money'. By postulating this ∅-head of N

---

[14] Although [X VN] act nominals are mostly used as VN's, they are also used as N, as shown below:
(i) kane-mooke o suru / (*kane o mookeru koto o suru)
    'to do profit-making' 'to do the act of profit-making'
(ii) kane-mooke wa tanosii./ (kane o mookeru koto wa tanosii)
    'profit-making is fun   the act of profit-making is fun
(i) shows the usage as VN, (ii) as N.

category and leaving the rest to an interpretation rule which applies according to the output semantic category lexically listed for each item (the category has to be lexically listed in any case), we can avoid the problems of deriving them from the relative clause source (see Makino 1976) and still maintain the generalizations.

(30) [kane-moti]VN ∅]N,Agent --> 'kane o motu hito'

This analysis is supported by the fact that sometimes the head is overtly realized as exemplified below.

(31) a. tume-kiri-basami (cf.29B) (nail-cut-scissors)
          'scissors for nails'
     b. mono-hosi-ba (29D) (thing-dry-place)
          'a place for drying laundry'
     c. hi-gure-doki (29E) (sun-set-time) 'senset time'

Now that we have claimed that all the [X VN] compounds are headed, we are left with the [VN N]VN compounds (25A) as the only case of the category mismatch. There is actually a well-motivated reason that this should be so. Namely, these compounds are formed by analogy to the Sino-Japanese (SJ) compounds which preserve the [V O] order of the source language, Chinese: ex. satu-zin (kill-person) 'murder' (cf. the native compound hito-gorosi (person-kill) 'murder'). Since SJ compounds occupy an important part in the vocabulary of Japanese it is not surprising that their word order influenced some of the native compounds.[15] The native

---

[15]Nishio (1976) gives the interesting observation that the V-O order of the SJ compounds cannot extend to the compounding of SJ compounds themselves, which always has the O-V order:
    satu-zin (kill-person) 'murder'

compounds of the form [VN N]VN are limited to the combination of V and DO, and even within that limit not very productive, compared with the [N VN] kind. It is only for this limited class of compounds, then, that we need to have a feature [+SJ], which assigns the left element to be the head. This feature is needed anyway for the interpretation of genuine SJ compounds. Consequently, we do not need to assume an unmotivated lexical reanalysis rule (28) proposed by Kageyama (1982). All Japanese compounds are right-headed except for the ones with the [+SJ] feature. This seems to be a natural result considering the fact that in Japanese all phrases are right-headed, because all arguments precede V and all modifiers precede the heads.[16]

---

   boo-si (prevent-stop) 'prevention'
   satuzin-boosi 'prevention of murder'
   *boosi-satuzin
This is due to the fact that each morpheme that forms a SJ compound (satu, zin, etc.) is largely bound, but the compound itself (satu-zin) is a free word. So the compounding of compounds is more transparent, and, unlike compounding of morphemes, can have a phrasal counterpart: satuzin no boosi, which naturally takes the O-V order. Incidentally, the compounding of SJ compounds is by far the most unrestricted form of WF process in Japanese (due to the lack of morphological ending and restrictions in combination). Okutsu (1975) gives an example of a SJ compound with 26 chinese morphemes.

[16]Bloomfield (1933: 14.5) discusses the classification of compounds with the terms 'syntactic' and 'asyntactic'; in syntactic compounds members 'stand to each other in the same grammatical relation as words in a phrase', while the members of asyntactic compounds 'stand to each other in a construction that is not paralleled in the style of their language'. Thus we can say for Japanese compounds with

Concluding the observations so far, we can say that one basic difference between English deverbal compounds and Japanese VN compounds is the lack of explicit suffixes in the latter which makes the semantics and usages of them less predictable by means of derivational rules.

2.1.3. Abstract nominals in VN compounds

Another noticeable difference between English deverbal compounds and their Japanese counterparts is the frequent occurrence of abstract nominals in the latter. Nominals derived from intransitive verbs are straightforward: <u>nemur-i</u> 'sleep', <u>aruk-i</u> 'walk', <u>oyog-i</u> 'swim', <u>wara-i</u> 'laugh', <u>odor-i</u> 'dance', and so on. On the other hand, nominals derived from transitive verbs are much less frequently used independently.[17] To illlustrate this point, let us consider the noun <u>writer</u> in English, as in a sentence:

---

deverbal nominals that they are mostly syntactic except for the ones with the [+SJ] feature.

[17] Besides appearing in compounds of the type discussed in the present section, a nominal derived from transitive verbs can combine with other deverbal nominals and form different types of compounds (cf. (18) (19)), in which case DO can be expressed with a genitive NP: hon no uri-kai 'selling and buying of books' (cf. *hon no kai, *hon no uri). It is suggested in Nishio (1961) that the single deverbal nominal in general is too 'unstable' in form and meaning to be independently used, because there is no suffix to indicate its meaning, and it is phonologically short (usually one or two syllables). This speculation, although it seems to be partially correct, does not explain the fact that the nominals derived from intransitive verbs are much more frequently used by themselves than those of transitive verbs.

(31) John's father is a famous writer.

Here DO of writing is unspecified and does not appear. This fact is pointed out and captured in Levi (1978: 5.3) by the rule of unspecified NP deletion, which deletes unspecified non-head NP's: in the case of writer, it deletes the theme argument x in WRITER [of x]. The theme argument may be expressed as a PP ('writer of this article') or in a deverbal compound ('song writer'), as we have already seen. The following are examples of VN compounds in Japanese where the DO is incorporated:

(32) uta-kaki 'song writer', syoosetu-kaki 'novelist' shibai-kaki 'playwright', kyakuhon-kaki 'script writer' komaasyaru-kaki 'commercial writer'

Now, unlike English, there is no form in Japanese that corresponds to an agent nominal with null theme argument, rather, the corresponding form is: mono-kaki (thing-write) 'writer'. This form is parallel to those in (32) except that the abstract noun mono is there to fill the theme argument slot without contributing any substantial meaning.

In the following some examples of mono- VN's are given, according to the position of the unspecified object in the case frame of the verb.

(33)
A. Accusative Object (x-ga y-o V)
a. mono-goi (thing-beg) 'begger, begging'
b. mono-uri (thing-sell) 'salesman'
c. mono-tori (thing-rob) 'robber, robbery'
d. mono-siri (thing-know) 'learned person'
e. mono-moti (thing-own) 'wealthy person'
f. mono-oboe (thing-memorize) 'memory'
g. mono-mane (thing-mimic) 'mimicry'
h. mono-osimi (thing-spare) 'being stingy'
i. mono-mi (thing-see) 'sight-seeing'

j. mono-omoi (thing-think)n 'meditation'

B. Dative object (x-ga y-ni V)
   a. mono-ozi (thing-be shy) 'being shy'
   b. mono-nare (thing-be accustomed) 'being accustomed'
   c. mono-aki (thing-be bored) 'being bored'

C. Nominative object (x-ni y-ga V)
   a. mono-iri (thing-need) 'being in need'
   b. mono-wakari (thing-understand) 'understanding'
   c. mono-zuki (thing-like) 'being curious
                           (lit. like strange things)'

As we can see from this list, these are all theme NP's, accusative NP's being the most frequent. Many of these are act nominals, and they often combine with <u>suru</u> 'do' to be used as a verb, in which case the verbal expression is quite similar in function to the 'intransitive use' of a transitive verb in English, as shown in the examples below:

(35) kare wa mono-goi o site kurasi-ta.
     he TOP begging ACC do live-PAST
     'He begged for a living.'

We can see that one function of these deverbal nominals in Japanese is to provide an 'intransitive' form (where the object NP is unspecified) for a transitive verb.

We noted above that there are two types of act nominals, [X VN] and [VN N], and that the latter is left-headed due to the analogy to SJ compounds. If the latter [VN N] compound is indeed a special case of deverbal nominal compound, we expect the abstract theme nominal to be functioning in the same way, and that is what we find. See the following examples.

(36) a. kaki-mono (write-thing) 'writing'
     b. kai-mono (buy-thing) 'shopping'
     c. ami-mono (knit-thing) 'kntting'
     d. arai-mono (wash-thing) 'washing, laundry'

e. okuri-mono (give-thing) 'gift-giving, gift'

Mono in these examples also indicates unspecified theme NP's. The fact that nominals in (34) and those in (36) are used on a par with each other despite the difference in the order of elements can be seen by the following passage taken from actual text, where they are conjoined by ya 'and'.

(37) Konogoro <u>otosi-mono ya mono-wasure</u> ga hagesiku,
recently lose-thing and thing-forgetNOM frequent

sagasi-mono o site ite mo nani o sagasite iru no ka
search-thingACCdoPROG even whatACC searchPROG COMP

wasurete simau.
forget completely

'Recently I frequently lose things and forget things, and even when I am looking for something, I forget what I was looking for.

It was mentioned a number of times in the preceding section that the deverbal compounds reflect the argument structure of the verb. It is not surprising that the difference between English <u>∅-writer</u> and Japanese <u>mono-kaki</u> is also found in the sentential structure, as shown below:

(38) a. He writes to earn a living.

b. Kare wa *(mono o) kaite kurasite iru.
he TOP   thingACC write live   PROG

Hence it is clear that the existence or non-existence of the rule on unspecified object deletion should be specified in the argument structure of the verb itself, rather than as a part of the nominal formation rule as done in Levi (1978).

The 'intransitive' use of a transitive verb with an unspecified object is discussed and accounted for by a rule of intransitivization in Bresnan (1982a) in the LFG framework. It assigns the null function to the object argument (ex. write (SU, ∅)), while not changing the predicate argument structure (write (Agent, Theme)), so that the null object argument is still existentially bound in the semantics. This type of rule is in contrast with another type of rules such as inchoativization, which alters the predicate argument structure: break (Agent, Theme) --> break (Theme). It can be said that while inchoativization changes the semantic valency of the verb, intransitivization leaves it unchanged. In Japanese, there seems to be no productive application of this intransitivization rule, and this is reflected in the form of deverbal compounds. Namely, the abstract nominal <u>mono</u> is used as a 'filler' for the unspecified object argument both in sentential structure and in compound structure. The fact that the intransitivization rule is not completely productive in English is seen from the use of the corresponding word <u>thing</u> in English in the following type of sentences, which are taken from Fronek (1982).

(39) a. She began to notice things.

   b. I am always forgetting things.   (V. Woolf)

It seems then that this opposition of formal (surface) transitivity is not as essential as the change in the predicate argument structure, as represented by the inchoativization rule. It is rather significant that in Japanese, while the intransitivization rule does not exist, the inchoative/transitive opposition is systematically marked by the verb morphology, unlike English: <u>kowas-u</u> ('break, tr.')/ <u>kowar-eru</u> ('break, intr.'), <u>yak-u</u> ('burn, tr.')/ <u>yak-eru</u> ('burn, intr.'), etc.[18] We can observe here that Japanese verb morphology is sensitive to and reflects the change in the verb's predicate argument structure, while English shows little morphology on the verb to reflect it. Another instance of such contrast is the 'causative' verb derived from an intransitive verb in English: John walks/ John walks his dog. The Japanese counterpart has a causative suffix: aruk-u / aruk-ase-ru. We may speculate that the absence of the intransitivization rule in Japanese as reflected in the form of deverbal compounds stems from the nature of Japanese verb morphology that it directly shows the valency of a verb, and hence, a rule that only changes the 'surface' transitivity of the verb such as the intransitivization rule does not exist for Japanese.

---

[18] See Jacobsen (1980) for a detailed account and discussion of this morphological opposition.

2.2. Suffixed deverbal nominals

2.2.1. Nominalization suffixes

In this section we will discuss a few suffixes that attach to the infinitive form of a verb to form a noun. (cf. 23b) One such suffix -te (a bound morpheme) makes an agent nominal, as exemplified below:

(40) a. oyogi-te 'swimmer'
    b. utai-te 'singer'
    c. kaki-te 'writer' (cf. mono-kaki)
    d. uri-te 'seller' (cf. mono-uri)

This formation of agent nominals differs in a number of ways from the compound formation of agent nominals (exemplified in 40c,d) that were discussed in the previous section. First, this process is productive and semantically transparent, unlike the compounds. Secondly, it can attach to activity verbs regardless of their transitivity. When a -te agent nominal is formed from a transitive verb, the object NP is either explicitly expressed by the genitive NP, or it has to be anaphorically understood in the discourse, while the compound agent nominals cannot have referential nouns incorporated. The following examples illustrate this point.

(41) a. Kare wa mono-kaki / *kaki-te da. 'He is a writer.'
        he TOP writer   writer COP

   b. Kare ga kono geki no *mono-kaki / kaki-te da.
      he NOM this play GEN   writer   writer COP
      'He is the writer of this play.'

c. Dare ga kono geki o kaita? 'Who wrote this play?'
   whoNOM this play ACC wrote
   Kare ga *mono-kaki / kaki-te da. 'He is the writer.
   he NOM writer   writer COP

In short, VN-<u>te</u> denotes the agent role of that verb, and when we use it we assume a certain activity that this agent is involved in, while <u>mono</u> + VN nominals denote a profession or an agent in a habitual action. The same thing can be said for a pair like <u>mono-uri</u> 'salesman' and <u>uri-te</u>; the former is somebody who makes a living by selling goods, while the latter is somebody who has something for sale.

In English there is one respect in which suffixed agent nominals and ∅-derived agent nominals have been noted to differ. The former systematically allows the realization of the theme argument by an of-phrase, while the latter does not. (If it does, it is idiosyncratic.)

(42) a. *the thief of the car
     b. the robber of the bank
     c. *the cook of the stew
        (cf. the cooking of the stew)

This was pointed out by Roeper (1983), where he attributes this difference to the presence of the affix, which, in his system, preserves the 'thematic grid' (i.e., assignment of the thematic roles) of the verb. The null suffix is not supposed to have this property. Roeper (1983) further speculates that it is the presence of certain suffixes such as <u>-er</u>, <u>-ing</u>, that enables the language learner to induce thematic roles associated with the source verb of the nominal, and thereby predict such differences as shown in

(42). Although this speculation has to be empirically tested on a wider range of data, it is interesting to note that we can find the same difference between suffixed agent nominals and compound agent nominals (as well as SJ compound agent nominals):

    (43) a. *sinario no mono-kaki 'writer of scenario'
            b. *sinario no sakka (SJ)
            c. sinario no kaki-te

Note that while English theme argument in (42) can also be realized in the compound structure, in Japanese only the compound nominal allows it:

    (44) a. car thief
            b. bank robber

            c. sinario-kaki 'scenario writer'
            d. sinario-sakka (SJ)
            e. *sinario-kaki-te

The fact shown by (44e) seems to hold even for a lexicalized -te agent nominal. So, utai-te generally means a professional singer (contrary to the general rule), but cannot make a compound in contrast with a SJ compound of the same meaning, kashu, which indicates that the unacceptability of (44e) is not due to the semantic inappropriateness of the second element for the compound structure.

    (45) a. zyazu no utai-te / *zyazu no kashu 'singer of jazz'
            b. *zyazu utai-te / zyazu-kashu 'jazz singer'

We will later discuss the difference between compounding and suffixation in some detail.

Going back to the question of the transparency in thematic role assignment, we can account for the facts in (42) above if we relate this suffixation to a noun modification structure. Namely, the following are equivalent:

(46) a. sinario no kaki-te 'writer of a scenario'

b. [sinario o kaku] hito 'person who writes scenarios'

We can view (46a) and (46b) as consisting of the same elements with the difference in the morphological nature of the head; one with a full noun, the other with a bound suffix.

(47) a. [sinario kak-]-te
b. [sinario kak-] hito

In (48a) below, since the head is a full noun, the verb is inflected as a finite form and the accusative case marking is also assigned. In (48b) the bound morpheme attaches to the VN (infinitive form) and accordingly the object argument takes a genitive marker, which is the case any NP must take in order to modify a noun.[19]

(48) a. [sinario o kaku] hito

b. [sinario no]NP [kaki-te]N

---

[19] If it is a grammatical argument (marked by *ga*, *o*, *ni* in a phrase), the NP simply takes the genitive marker *no*, but if it is an oblique argument such as *kara* 'from', *e* 'to', *made* 'until', and so on, the genitive marker attaches to the postposition: Tookyo kara no kyaku 'guest from Tokyo' (cf. *Tookyo kara kyaku).

According to our rule typology, the formation of (48) must be syntactic, while (48ab) differ in that (48a) involves only a phrasal operation and (48b) involves both phrasal and morphological operations. This analysis captures the parallel compositionality between (48a) and (48b) and at the same time the difference in their forms.

One might argue that by assuming that the suffix -te preserves the thematic role assignment of the verb, we can capture the same parallelism, and then we can contend that the suffixed agent nominals and compound agent nominals both belong to the lexicon except that they differ on this point. There are several reasons why this is not a satisfactory move. First, there is the semantic transparency and the productivity of the suffixed agent nominals as opposed to the compound nominals, although it is not a decisive piece of evidence, given the lack of clarity of notions like 'productivity'. Secondly, the fact that this nominal cannot enter a compound as mentioned above (44, 45) suggests that this suffixation is a different type of derivation from the ∅-nominalization and the compound formation. Our assumption that this suffixation is a syntactic rule while the ∅-nominalization and the compound formation are lexical rules is consistent with this observation. (See below for more discussion on this point.) Thirdly, the most revealing piece of evidence is the occurrence of this suffix with a certain type of V'. The type of phrase that appears with the agent nominal suffix -te is [x-ni nar-] 'become x', where x is a subcategorized complement of the verb. Although this verb 'naru' appears with two NP's, SU and the complement x, the verb forms a tighter unit with the complement than with SU.[20] This makes sense when we consider that the complement is not a grammatical argument of the verb in the way subject and object are. Thus 'naru' is not a transitive verb even though it occurs with two NP's. When the suffix -te attaches to this verb, the complement remains unchanged, as shown in the following examples.

(49) a. Kare wa [yome ni nari]-te o sagasite-iru.
       he TOP brideCOPbecome ACC look for-PROG
       'He is looking for a bride-to-be.'

b. Inaka dewa [isya ni nari]-te ga sukunai.
   countryLOC doctorCOPbecome NOM few
   'Few become a doctor in a rural town.'

Note that the bracketing [yome ni] [nari-te] is not a possible configuration in Japanese, since an NP modifying a noun must take the genitive marker. (See fn. 19) In addition, there are cases cited in Martin (1975: 224) which involve a phrasal concatenation of verbs, 'V-te kureru' ('do a favor of V-ing'):

---

[20]This point can be demonstrated by the fact that the complement NP resists scrambling to the S-initial position, while other grammatical arguments or adverbs do not:
(i) Taroo wa isya ni nat-ta. 'Taroo became a doctor.'
      TOP doctorCOP become-PAST
(ii) ??Isya ni Taroo wa nat-ta.
The marker 'ni' on the complement is the adverbial form (ren-yoo-kei) of the copula.

(50) a. [Aite ni site kure]-te ga nakat-ta.
          companyCOPmake give   NOM NEG-PAST
      'Nobody would be my company.'

   b. [Moratte kure]-te ga arimasen.
       take   give   NOM be-NEG (polite)
      'Nobody would take it.'

In (50a) 'suru'(site) is the causative counterpart of 'naru'. These phrases never find their way into compound structures, but with this suffix and several other ones (as shown below), they are rather frequent. This fact indicates that the domain of some nominal suffixes can expand in certain cases beyond the lexical level.[21]

The preceding observations lead us to conclude that the agent nominal suffixation is a morphological-syntactic process as opposed to the compound formation which is morphological-lexical, and the former can interact with some phrasal-syntactic processes, as illustrated in the chart below according to our rule typology.

---

[21]One conceivable alternative way of dealing with such cases as (49) and (50) is to claim that the complement is 'inherited' under the nominalization process. Moortgat (1983) attempts to provide the compositional semantics for the complement inheritance cases in English (e.g., John's willingness to please; John's kindness to Mary) by introducing a new function in the semantics which allows -ness to have scope over the infinitive or the PP while adhering to the lexicalist assumption that the suffix attaches only to the adjective in the word formation. We will discuss this approach in Chapter III in comparison with the phrasal suffixation approach that we adopt. It suffices to note here that while the English cases exemplified here do not build any new structure (they are [[NP] [PP]]NP), the Japanese cases discussed above do, due to the strict morphological condition that all the prenominal modifier NPs must take the genitive marker (see fn. 19.)

(51)

	syntactic	lexical
phrasal:	[SF o kaku] hito [yome ni naru] hito	
morph'l:	[SF no] [kaki-te] [yome ni nari]-te	SF-kaki, SF-sakka

The assumption that the lexical rules generally precede syntactic rules is consistent with the fact that the compound of VN's, which are [+N], cannot feed the agent suffixation, since only the infinitive form of a verb can be suffixed.

(52) a. yomi-kaki 'reading and writing' --> *yomi-kaki-te
 b. SF-kaki 'SF writing' --> *SF-kaki-te
 c. hasiri-gaki (run-write) 'scribble'
  --> *hasiri-gaki-te
 (cf. uke-toru V. 'receive' --> uke-tori-te)

On the other hand, since a syntactically derived word can be lexicalized, it is possible for the agent suffixation nominal to acquire a special meaning (cf. utai-te 'professional singer') or to feed the compound formation (cf. kai-te sizyoo 'buyer's market.)[22]

There are several other nominalization suffixes that attach to the infinitive form of the verb, and they behave in the same way as the agent suffix, as far as the facts discussed here are concerned. They are exemplified below, along with their phrasal counterpart; some of them can also

---

[22] As noted earlier, some compound formation is more transparent and productive than others. One productive type is the act nominal formation by the incorporation of DO, and a compound such as the following seems to be acceptable:
 (i) sinario no kaki-te sagasi 'sinario-writer-to-be search'

be used as a free word as indicated in the parentheses.

(53) -kata 'the manner of V-ing, how to V'
 a. hon no yomi-kata 'how to read books'
    bookGENread-way

 b. hon o yomu hoohoo

(54) -kai (also a free word) 'the value of'
 a. kenkyuu no si-gai 'the worthiness of research'
    researchGENdo-value

 b. kenkyuu o suru kai

(55) -sama 'the manner, appearance of' (also a free word)
 a. iki-zama 'the way a person lives'
    live

 b. ikiru sama

(56) -sama 'on the point (in time) on V-ing'
 a. booru no suimen ni ukiagari-zama (o tataku)
    ball GEN surfaceLOC float-point (ACC hit)
    'hit the ball when it comes up to the surface'

 b. booru ga suimen ni ukiagaru tokoro (o tataku)

One suffix '-yoo' has an interesting distribution in that it leaves the accusative marker on DO unchanged when it is used as part of the fixed expression -yoo ga nai 'there is no V-ing' as shown below:

(57) a. kane no / *o tukai-yoo o kangaeru.
      moneyGEN ACC use-way ACC think
      'think about how to spend money'

 b. kane no / o tukai-yoo ga nai
    moneyGEN ACC use-way NOM be-NEG
    'there is no way of spending money'

In (57b) when the accusative marker is also acceptable, the expression -yoo ga nai is very likely reanalyzed as an auxiliary with the meaning 'cannot'.

These examples show how a nominal suffixation can be close (in derivation and perception) to a phrasal noun modification structure, in contrast with the compound formation. Classifying the former as syntactic and the latter as lexical, despite their both being morphological, can capture this difference nicely.

2.2.2. Deverbal nominals of ambiguous status

We have just mentioned one suffix -yoo, which can occur with a V' (NP o V-inf.-yoo) as well as a N' (NP no V-inf.-yoo) when it is part of the fixed expression -yoo ga nai. There exists a more frequent and productive type of construction with a similar property, as exemplified below:

(58) a. oyogi ni iku 'go swimming'
b. asobi ni kuru 'come to play'
c. kowasi ni kakaru 'set about to destroy'

Morphologically, the verb form (of the first element) is ambiguous between an infinitive and a noun. What follows this VN ('ni') is a postposition indicating purpose or goal, and from that point of view the verb form is functioning as a noun on a par with the nouns in the following examples:

(59) a. paatii ni iku 'go to a party'
b. heya ni kuru 'come to a room'
c. ronbun ni kakaru 'start on a paper'

On the other hand, what is peculiar about these constructions is that the verb can appear with its argument and complement (without the morphological change on them to modify a noun):

(60) a. puuru de oyogi ni iku 'go swimming in the pool'
     b. kodomo to asobi ni kuru 'come to play with children'
     c. biru o kowasi ni kakaru 'start destroying a building'

If the VN form is really a noun, all the complements and arguments must be accompanied by the genitive marker, as has been mentioned previously, but that is not possible here:

(61) a. *puuru de-no oyogi ni iku
     b. *kodomo to-no asobi ni kuru
     c. *biru no kowasi ni kakaru

We saw that VN compounds and the infinitive forms have almost a complementary distribution in regard to compound formation and nominal suffixation, but in this construction that difference does not figure.[23]

(62) a. yama ni nobori ni iku
        mount.GO climb   go
     b. yama-nobori ni iku   'go mountain-climbing'

(63) a. ueki ni mizu o yari ni iku 'go to water plants'
        plantDATwaterACCgive go
     b. ueki no mizu-yari ni iku

(64) a. mado o huki ni kakaru 'start cleaning windows'
        wind.ACCclean   start
     b. mado-huki ni kakaru 'start window-cleaning'

SJ compounds are completely ambiguous, since they all have both verbal and nominal usages (unlike native VN's), and they allow both patterns:

(65) a. gakkoo o/no sisatu ni iku 'go inspect schools'

---

[23]On the other hand, the two (compound and phrase) cannot mix in one configuration, as shown:
(i) a. mizuumi de oyogi ni iku. 'go swimming in the lake'
    b.*mizuumi de sakana-turi ni iku.'go fishing in the lake'
       lake   LOC fish -catch   go
    (cf. mizuumi de sakana o turi ni iku.)
         lake LOC fish ACC catch   go

      b. kekka o/no hookoku ni kuru 'come to report the result'
      c. heya o/no soozi ni kakaru 'start cleaning the room'

In these particular constructions, it seems as though the VN's have two different faces. To its left, it combines with its arguments and modifiers as a verb, while to its right it is followed by a case marker as a noun. There is no doubt that the morphological ambiguity between the nominal form and the infinitive (verbal) form enables this ambiguity, but we should also note that we find this kind of phenomena also with some cases of suffixation. It is likely that the agglutinative mode of concatenation in Japanese is one factor behind such cases. We have seen above one case of suffixation that involves a phrase in an example like <u>yome ni nari-te</u> 'bride-to-be'. Another way of conceiving of this case would be to say that the complement 'yome ni' combines syntactically with 'nar-' (V), which, in turn morphologically combines with a nominalization suffix. Each combination is well-formed in the language; it is just that as a whole this construction does not fit the regular configuration of Japanese. We will discuss more examples in the following chapters, but it is to be noted here that such variety in the distribution of the VN form of a verb casts a question as to what is a genuine case of nominalization as part of derivational morphology.

3. A note on the condition on rendaku

In the preceding section we have seen numerous examples of compounds in which the initial voiceless consonant of the second element is changed to a voiced consonant under the compound formation. This phenomenon, referred to as 'rendaku', has been long noted, although the exact condition of its application has not been clarified. Actually, it has been claimed by those who investigated the process in great details that it is largely unsystematic and idiosyncratic (Martin 1952, Vance 1979). It will be pointed out in this section that the consideration of the different morphological concatenations can give us some insights into the nature of this process.

There are two generalizations over the application of this process that have been attested to hold. One is known as 'Lyman's Law', attributed to Lyman (1894), although the observation is claimed to go further back to Norinaga Motoori in the 18th C, according to Vance (1979). Lyman's Law says that if there already is a voiced consonant contained anywhere in the second element, rendaku is blocked. For instance, kaki'oyster' gets rendaku (nama-gaki'raw oyster', while kagi'key' never does (ai-kagi). This condition is almost exceptionless, and only a few counterexamples have been found so far. The other well-known generalization is the non-occurrence of rendaku in dvandva compounds. It is this generalization that we will take a closer look here. Three lexical categories of [+N] can form dvandva compounds, and they are exemplified below along with their ordinary compound counterparts.

(66) N-N: oya-ko 'parent and child'
(cf. sato-go 'foster child'
mai-go 'lost child')

eda-ha 'branches and leaves'
(cf. waka-ba 'young leaves'
futa-ba 'seed (lit. two) leaves')

V-V: yuki-kaeri 'coming and going'
(cf. Amerika-gaeri 'returnee from America'
hi-gaeri 'day trip (lit. return)')

yomi-kaki 'read and write'
(cf. te-gaki 'hand written'
hasiri-gaki 'quick-written')

AN-AN: siro-kuro 'black and white'
(cf. iro-guro 'dark (lit. color-black)')

What distinguishes dvandva compounds from the other compounds is the lack of modifying relationship between the two elements. Ordinary compounds are generally right-headed, with the first element modifying or specifying the second element in some way. The accent pattern roughly corresponds to this difference, although the accent patterns for different types of compounds vary in subtle ways. Namely, dvandva compounds retain the accent of the first element and erase the rest, while in ordinary compounds the accent of the second element dominates the pattern: yomi-kaki vs. te-gaki. We are led to hypothesize that rendaku reflects the modifying relationship between the two elements in the compound; just as the accent pattern marks the head of the ordinary compounds (X $\widehat{Y}$), the voicing marks the second element as the head.

In addition to this well-discussed condition on the application of rendaku just discussed, there are two significant tendencies we find with this process. One significant contrast can be found among the compounds with deverbal nominals (that were discussed in Section 2). The second element of these compounds resist rendaku considerably when the first element is a noun and stands in DO relation to the base verb of the second element, as opposed to when the first element is an adjective/adverb or a noun with oblique relations. The following examples illustrate this observation.

(67) a. e-kaki (picture-paint) 'painter'
   te-gaki (hand-paint) 'hand painted'
   sita-gaki (under-write) 'draft'

b. mesi-taki (rice-cook) 'rice cooking'
   mizu-daki (water-cook) 'casserole'
   kara-daki (empty-cook) 'putting an empty pan on fire'

c. mono-hosi (thing-dry) 'place for drying laundry'
   kage-bosi (shade-dry) 'drying in the shade'

d. syakkin-tori (loan-collect) 'loan collector'
   yoko-dori (side-take) 'snatch'

e. sakana-turi (fish-catch) 'fishing'
   iso-zuri (beach-fishing) 'fishing on the beach'

The contrast in the relationship of the two elements in these compounds can be stated as the following. While DO and a verb stand in argument-predicate relationship and they together name an action, an oblique noun or adjective/adverb and a verb stand in modification relationship by which a certain kind of act is restricted to its subkind.[24] Thus it seems possible to extend the hypothesis we made about the contrast between dvandva compounds and ordinary nominal compounds to this case as well. Namely, rendaku most readily applies where the two elements in a complex word stand in modification relationship, where 'modification' excludes the predicate-argument relationship.

There is another significant contrast found with verbal/adjectival compounds. The compounds discussed so far all belong to [+N] category. There are compounds formed with the [+V] head as well, in which case the first element can be N, AN (adjective stem), VN, or a prefix. An interesting contrast exists between VN-V / AN-A compounds and the rest; the former resist rendaku to a significantly greater extent than the latter. Especially, the Japanese lexicon abounds in X-V compounds (unlike English), and it is

---

[24] What remains a puzzle here is that the same contrast cannot clearly be found with SU-VN compounds, which should behave parallel to DO- VN compounds. Although there are some cases with this contrast (i.e., ame-huri 'rainfall' / hon-buri 'heavy rainfall'), many SU-VN compounds seem to show rendaku (cf. yuki-doke (snow-melt), hi-gure (sun-set)). Further, when the second element of a DO-VN compound consists of three syllables, it shows rendaku more frequently. So, although we have a contrast such as mahoo-tukai (magic-user, witch), hebi-tukai (snake-dancer) / hasiri-zukai (run-use 'errand person'), we also have yama-biraki (mountain-open), hito-gorosi (kill-person)'murder', and so on. It is more than likely that the fact that the first syllable of the second element in these compounds is accented (yama-bi̇raki) as opposed to the ones in (67) above (mono̜hosi) is one factor behind this difference. These problems remain for future research.

with these compounds that the contrast is most clear. The following gives examples of the compounds formed with two fairly productive verbs and one adjective. (Gloss is given for only a few representative ones, since many of them have rather subtle meanings that would take many words to translate.)

(68) a. tatu 'stand' 'leave, depart'

    VN-V: ikiri-tatu, uki-tatu, omoi-tatu, ori-tatu, kiri-tatu, sosori-tatu, takeri-tatu, tut-tatu, ture-datu, tobi-tatu, nari-tatu, ni-tatu, nie-tatu, hiki-tatu, hurui-tatu, yuki-tatu, moe-tatu 'flare up', waki-tatu 'boil'.

    N-V: awa-datu 'foam', ukiasi-datu, ozike-datu, ozoke-datu, omote-datu, kasira-datu, kado-datu, kiwa-datu, keba-datu, saki-datu, sakki-datu, su-datu, sooke-datu, tabi-datu 'leave on a trip' tuno-datu, tunome-datu, tubu-datu, tuma-datu, tumasaki-datu, toge-datu, nami-datu, hara-datu, hi-datu, hukure-datu, mimi-datu.

    AN-V: ara-datu, omo-datu, saka-datu.

b. kiru 'cut' 'stop' 'do x entirely'

    VN-V: ii-kiru, uti-kiru 'put an end' osi-kiru omoi-kiru, kai-kiru, kasi-kiru, kak-kiru kari-kiru, kui-kiru 'bite off', si-kiru sime-kiru, sumi-kiru, suri-kiru, dasi-kiru tati-kiru, tate-kiru, tuki-kiru, tume-kiru de-kiru, nigari-kiru, nezi-kiru, nori-kiru hasami-kiru, hari-kiru, humi-kiru, huri-kiru mi-kiru, moti-kiru, yaki-kiru, wari-kiru

    N-V: ura-giru, ku-giru 'divide up' se-giru, ne-giru ma-giru, yoko-giru 'cut across'

c. kurusii (A) 'hard' 'difficult' 'suffocating'

    AN-A: atu-kurusii 'hot and stifling' omo-kurusii kata-kurusii, sema-kurusii, musa-kurusii

    N-A: iki-gurusii, muna-gurusii, kokoro-gurusii,

    VN-A: kiki-gurusii, mi-gurusii, ne-gurusii

Nishio and Miyajima (1971) has a list of frequently used verbal and adjectival compounds. Counting the number of cases where rendaku takes place in each category gives us the following figures; the figures after the slash are the number of the potential cases of rendaku, namely, where other phonological conditions such as the first consonant being capable of changed to a voiced consonant and the Lyman's Law discussed above are met.

  VN-V compounds: 11/667

  N-V compounds: 142/154

  AN-V compounds: 10/10

The figures for adjectival compounds are not as clear cut. First, it seems hard to distinguish AN-A compounds from prefix-A; for instance, usu- 'thin' in usu-gurai 'slightly dark' seems to be functioning as a prefix rather than an adjective, especially since the lexical meaning is not preserved. Secondly, there is one adjective kusai 'stinky' which resists rendaku in general, but is very productive with nouns to form a compound with the meaning roughly translated as 'smelling like x'. We will list this item separately below.

  AN-A compounds: 6/13

  VN-A compounds: 9/9 (-kusai: 0/1)

  N-A compounds: 43/47 (-kusai: 2/25)

  Prefix-A: 11/12

The correlation we find with adjectives is only one-way here: if the first element of X-A compound is not AN, the frequency of rendaku is very high (except for the lexical exception of -kusai).

So far we have put forward the hypothesis that rendaku tends to apply to compounds in which the elements stand in modification relationship. It is not immediately clear how we can extend it to account for this contrast just mentioned. If we examine the headedness of these compounds, however, we notice some interesting points. The [+N] compounds we have seen are clearly right-headed except for the dvandva compounds. Now looking at the verbal/adjectival compounds, we see that when a verb or an adjective is compounded on its left with a morpheme of a category other than its own (including prefix), the resulting compound is clearly right-headed in that it is the second element that determines the lexical category of the word as a whole. On the other hand, VN-V compounds and AN-A compounds are not clearly right-headed in this sense, since neither of the two items can be regarded as determining the category of the whole word. In terms of semantics, on the other hand, it is not clear that they are non-headed (or bi-headed) as dvandva compounds because they cannot always be paraphrased by 'X and X'. In fact, among the numerous VN-V compounds, the semantics vary: it can be a conjunction 'V and V' (ex. tobi-haneru 'jump and hop'); the second element can be subordinate (ex. moe-tatu 'flare up'); or the first element can be subordinate (ex. tori-kaeru (take-change) 'exchange'); and in many cases it is quite difficult to determine the semantic head. It seems plausible to speculate, then, that this lack of (clear) headedness is responsible for the fact that these compounds resist rendaku. The contrast between DO and oblique nouns that we found with deverbal nominal compounds above is not easy to spot with N-V compounds, but it is rather significant that among the 12 'exception' cases of N-V compounds not showing rendaku (while 143 N-V compounds do), 9 of them consist of DO and V. On the other hand, many N-V compounds with DO show rendaku. (Also see the following footnote.)

The observations made in this section can be summed up as the following. Rendaku applies most readily to a compound XY if X modifies Y and Y is the semantic as well as lexical head of the compound. The notion 'modification' here stands in contrast with 'argument-predicate' relation especially that of DO and V. Rendaku, then, can be seen as a way of marking the head of a complex word. It is further conceivable that by marking the head and reflecting the modification relationship between the morphemes that make up a complex word, rendaku actually has the function of marking the complex word as a lexical and semantic unit, in a language where phrasal and morphological concatenations are sometimes obscured in form.[25] In an agglutinative language such as Japanese, rendaku is one of the few phonological processes triggered by word formation. It is therefore not surprising that we find some morphological conditions as well as motivations in the application of this process, despite its often-remarked idiosyncracy to some extent.

---

[25] In this respect the tendency found with N-V compounds that do not show rendaku is interesting. Namely, many of them seem to be in between a word and a N-V sequence with a case marking dropped, and do not seem to form a very tight unit as a word compared to the other N-V compounds. They are typically compositional and transparent in their meanings. For instance, compare kosi-kakeru (buttock-put) 'sit' (same in meaning as kosi o kakeru) with te-gakeru (hand-put) 'start or try (a project)', or tosi-toru (age-take) 'to age' (same in meaning as tosi o toru with ke-doru (sense-take) 'notice'. See Kageyama (1977) for the discussion on 'post-cyclic' noun incorporation versus 'pre-cyclic' noun incorporation.

CHAPTER III

ARGUMENT STRUCTURE AND DERIVATIONAL MORPHOLOGY
OF ADJECTIVES

This chapter will examine derivational morphology involving adjectives as base. We discussed in the previous chapter the important role that argument structure of verbs plays in regulating the formation and the distribution of deverbal nominals. Although argument structure of adjectives has attracted less attention compared with that of verbs, we will see below that it is essential for capturing the regularities that adjectives exhibit in morphological derivation, as we will see. In fact, since there is a completely productive and transparent nominalization suffix for Japanese adjectives (unlike verbs), it turns out that the examination of deadjectival nominals can yield some fruitful results for determining the argument structure of different types of adjectives and the surface constituent structure of the sentences containing them.

In section 1 general problems regarding argument structure of adjectives in English will be discussed, followed by discussion on how argument structure is reflected in the nominalization and the compound formation of adjectives. In Section 2 we will discuss two kinds of nominalizing suffixes for Japanese adjectives, and will point out some theoretical consequences of the observation made about them. Section 3 will examine the verbalizing suffix <u>-garu</u>, which has some interesting properties.

1. Argument structure of English adjectives

1.0. English adjectives have not been discussed in much detail in terms of their argument structure compared to verbs. It is because many adjectives are basically one-place predicates (Theme, A) and when they subcategorize for a complement, it takes the form of PP with a lexically specified P (ex. [NP, of NP], [NP, to NP]), thus A', unlike V', does not contain NP.[1]

On the other hand, the basic intransitive nature of adjectives, as opposed to verbs, (i.e., that they can subcategorize only for PP's in English) has been questioned by Riemsdijk (1980) from the point of view of universal grammar. Namely, the fact that English adjectives do not generally subcategorize for NP's is reflected in GB framework in the assumption of the case theory that adjectives ([+N]) do not assign case. Riemsdijk (1980) points out that German adjectives can subcategorize for

---

[1] There are three exceptions, as noted in McCawley (1982): <u>worth</u>, <u>like</u>, and <u>near</u>. See Maling (1980) for discussion on the synchronic status of them. It is claimed by Maling that while <u>near</u> passes most of the tests for being an adjective, the other two words behave more like prepositions than adjectives.

dative or genitive marked NP's, and thus German adjectives must be allowed to have the case-assigning property. To this effect he proposes a neutralization of syntactic features ([+V, +N] -> [+V]) for German.

It is thus plausible to state here that the question of how the generalizations over case pattern and argument structure of adjectives should be captured is still an open one in universal grammar.

1.1. Complement inheritance under nominalization

A number of English adjectives can preserve their complements under nominalization. The following are some examples:

(1) eager to succeed ---> eagerness to succeed
    distinct from x ---> distinctness from x
    familiar with x ---> familiarity with x
    kind to Mary ---> kindness to Mary
    important to x ---> importance to x

It has been pointed out (cf. Moortgat (1983)) that these cases (among others) present a problem to the assumption of functional composition in the framework of syntactic operation where word-building always precedes phrase-building. Namely, although the nominalizing suffixes such as -ness and -ity attach to an adjective alone, their semantic scope in these cases clearly includes the entire A' (eager to succeed, etc.). Rather than loosening the constraints on the syntactic operation of word grammar (i.e., the strict lexicalist restriction), Moortgat opts for a reworking of the semantics that accompany these expressions so that the proper scope of the suffixes is ensured in the semantics. We are not concerned here with the technical details of how this is done. Rather, what we will be questioning are: what kind of restrictions exist for this type of 'complement inheritance' phenomena; and whether there is any difference in the empirical consequences between the postulation of 'complement inheritance' and that of phrasal suffixation that we have already proposed.

We will first consider the generalizations over the correspondence between the following expressions:

(2) a. X is A PP / to VP

b. X's A-suff.(N) PP/ to VP

Although the correspondence between (2a) and (2b) seems to be a fairly general one, as exemplified in (1), it is not completely so, as illustrated below:

(3) a. John is familiar with the problem.

John's familiarity with the problem.

b. The problem is familiar to John.

*the problem's familiarity to John.

(4) a. The job was easy for John.

*the job's easiness for John.

(5) a. The car was precious to Mary.

*the car's preciousness to Mary.

We can see that it is not the subcategorization features nor the particular suffixes that rule out the particular cases of nominalizations such as the ones above.

It has been noted since early days of generative grammar that some verbs (especially 'psychological' predicates) do not undergo regular nominalization but rather what might be described as 'passive' nominalization:

(6) a. John amused Mary.
    b. *John's amusement of Mary.
    c. Mary's amusement at John.
       (cf. Mary was amused at John.)

Based on this fact and other similar cases, Amritavalli (1980) argues against the assumption in X' theory that cross-categorial correspondence between S and NP can be expressed using grammatical functions only. She notes that these verbs that behave 'irregularly' under nominalization have NP's with the thematic functions of Experiencer as DO position, and proposes that argument structure be used in expressing cross-categorial correspondence. Amritavalli illustrates this claim by a triangle diagram of V, N, and A with their respective argument structures and corresponding subcategorizations.

(7)
```
                        V
                (Causer, Experiencer)
                 SU NP       DO NP

         N                         A
   (Experiencer, X)         (Experiencer, X)
    Poss.NP    PP            SU NP      PP
```

This diagram is supposed to represent three different directions of derivations as exemplified by: amuse(V) -> amused(A), amusement(N); sad(A) -> sadden(V), sadness(N); terror(N) -> terrify(V), terrified(A). There exist other derivational relations between these categories, but the point Amritavalli (1980) tries to make is that argument structure of the verb is not paralllel to that of N or A for these triples, and thus the cross-categorial correspondence between S and NP based on subcategorzations breaks down. What is interesting for our discussion here is the fact that the correspondence between A and N as represented in the diagram reflects a type of nominalization under which the complements of adjectives are inherited. On the other hand, it seems to be generally the case that when an adjective take its theme argument as subject and the experiencer argument as PP, this PP cannot be preserved under nominalization. Take the contrast shown in (4) above, repeated here:

(8) a. John is familiar with the problem.

John's familiarity with the problem.

b. The problem is familiar to John.

* The problem's familiarity to John.

In terms of subcategorization, both (8a) and (8b) take [NP, PP], but in their argument structure (8a) has [Exp. Theme], while (8b) has [Theme, Exp.]. Further, note that for (8a) the PP is obligatory, while for (8b) can be absent in a sentence in which case an understood or arbitrary Experiencer is implied. This is partially similar to the realization of Agent/Theme arguments with derived nominals.

(9) a. the enemy's destruction *(of the city)

b. the city's destruction (by the enemy)

As pointed out in Roeper (1983), the theme argument can invoke the implicit agent (cf. 9b), but not vice versa (cf. 9a). It can further be pointed out that in that sense the genitive NP position is more central than the PP position. Similarly, we can say for (4a,b) that the theme of an adjective can imply an implicit experiencer, while an experiencer cannot invoke an implicit theme. What differs between (4) and (7) is that the Experiencer PP cannot be present under nominalization (cf.(4b)) while the Agent PP can. Why there exists such a difference is not clear to me at this point, but the facts indicate that for nominalizaton of adjectives there is a hierarchy of thematic relations: Experiencer > Theme > others. Coupled with the assumption that the genitive NP is more central than the PP in the nominalization construction, we can predict that the thematic functions can appear in the following way.

(10)   NP's   A-suff.   PP

   [Exp.   Theme   ]

   [Theme   oblique]

  *[Theme   Exp   ]

  *[Oblique   Theme   ]

This predicts the unacceptability of (3b), (4b) and (5b) as opposed to (3a) as well as the phrases in (1) above.[2]

Besides this problem of what kind of complements can be inherited, thematic functions seem to also regulate the choice of the genitive NP in the nominalization of certain adjectives. Consider the following:

(11) a. John was sad.

   John's sadness

   b. The movie was sad.

   *the movie's sadness

(12) a. John is cold.

   *John's coldness (not the personality sense)

   b. the room is cold.

   the room's coldness

What is puzzling here is that in (11) the theme argument cannot be realized by the genitive phrase as opposed to the experiencer, while in (12) the situation is the opposite. One possibility is that although these adjectives occur with NP's of more than one thematic functions as their subject, one thematic function is more basic than the other, and the nominalization disambiguates this. With _sad_ it is easy to see that the experiencer is more basic than the theme; for one thing, the use of _sad_ in (11b) does not extend to its

---

[2]Here we are ignoring the problem of how to assign thematic functions to each NP and PP. Although it is a serious and important problem that has been noted by many, it is beyond our concern in this study.

antonyms happy, glad, etc. On the other hand, cold shows the opposite pattern, and with this and other temperature adjectives it is not clear which, if either, of thematic functions is more basic. One can also note that sad in the sense used in (11b) implies an implicit experiencer while cold in (12b) does not, but how that is related to the pattern of nominalization as shown here remains unsolved. It is at least clear that mere subcategorization features cannot predict this pattern, and we would very likely need to make use of argument structure in accounting for these facts.

Let us go back to the discussion of complement inheritance. We have seen that what complements can be preserved under nominalization is determined largely by the thematic functions they carry. It is not, however, determined solely by the specific suffixes, contrary to what is stated in Moortgat (1981), where he classifies affixes into two classes according to their transparency in terms of complement inheritance. Another fact about the data we have seen here is that the suffixes that figure in these cases belong to different levels in the level-ordered approach to morphology. Namely, -ness belong to level 2, while -ity and -ance belong to level 1. This implies that the phonological transparency and idiosyncracy are not relevant as property of the transparent suffixes. This is one feature that may distinguish the cases of phrasal suffixation from complement inheritance cases. Phrasal suffixation, as conceived here, involves only a specific set of suffixes that are productive and show little idiosyncracy. The cases of complement inheritance found with adjective nominalization do not share this property. We will discuss further differences between the two later in this chapter.

1.2. Adjectival compounds

So far we have discussed the importance of argument structure of adjectives in accounting for the facts about nominalization. Turning our eyes to adjectival compounds, we also find that argument structure is playing a crucial role, contrary to what has been claimed. Specifically, it is claimed in Lieber (1983) that among the lexical categories of N, A, V, and P, the latter two (V, P) are argument-taking while the former two (N, A) are not. She thus predicts that the compounds formed with N and A (NN, NA, AN, AA) are not restricted in any way, since the argument linking principle (ALP) does not apply (see Chapter 2 for the description of ALP.) This is in contrast with the compounds with deverbal elements, to which ALP applies. Lieber (1983) says that a compound of this type 'will never be ruled out on the ground that one of its stems cannot satisfy its argument structure.' This remark seems to hold, however, only for the use of the one-place adjectives in compound structure. Consider the following examples of possible NA compounds given in Lieber (1983):

(13) sky-blue, girl-crazy, color-blind, branch-brown,
wife-blind, gun-crazy

We immediately notice that there are two types of NA compounds. One type has a noun modifying the adjective with a meaning 'A like N'. The examples sky-blue and branch-brown above are of this type, and so are pitch-dark, razor-sharp, paper-thin, etc. On the other hand, consider color-blind, gun-crazy, and girl-crazy above, as well as such compounds as class-conscious, light-sensitive, water-resistant, blood-thirsty, user-friendly (as seen in a computer advertisement), and so on. The relationship of N and A here is not that of modification but rather that of argument-predicate. Namely, adjectives such as sensitive, and crazy differ from blue and thin in that they can take 'object' (in a broad sense) PP, and it is with the noun of this PP that they form a compound. This seems to be quite parallel to the way verbal compounds such as truck-driver and church-goer are formed. Further, we understand these adjectival compounds not in any arbitrary way, but we relate them to the appropriate adjectival phrase such as conscious of class, crazy about girls, and so on. Similarly a new compound can be formed based on adjectival phrases--for instance, see the following line taken from a newspaper.

(14) Rain pounded the water-weary Midwest on this day . . .

(Chicago Tribune, June, 1984.)

Here again, <u>water</u> is the oblique argument of <u>weary</u> (<u>weary</u> <u>of</u> <u>water</u>) and this information about the argument structure of <u>weary</u> is crucial in understanding this new compound. Thus, in a way, adjectives also form compounds with their first sister element in A'. (See Chapter II for the discussion of the first sister principle on verbal compounds.) Note that for the compound <u>girl-crazy</u>, it is not possible to assign an interpretaton that 'girl are crazy about x'.

The other type, namely the modification type NA compounds ('A like N') can be said to be obeying the FSP as well, since in an adjectival phrase <u>blue</u> <u>like</u> <u>the</u> <u>sky</u>, <u>like</u> <u>the</u> <u>sky</u> can be regarded as the first sister to A, just as for the verbal compound <u>hand-painted</u>, <u>by</u> <u>hand</u> of <u>paint</u> <u>by</u> <u>hand</u> is the first sister element. This observation predicts that the modification type NA compounds contain only one-place adjectives, and this prediction seems to be borne out. The compound <u>girl-crazy</u> can either mean <u>crazy</u> <u>about</u> <u>girls</u> or <u>crazy</u> <u>like</u> <u>girls</u>, but not <u>crazy</u> <u>about</u> <u>something</u> <u>like</u> <u>girls</u>.

We can conclude by saying that contrary to what Lieber (1983) claims, the possible formation and interpretation of NA compounds are restricted by the argument structure of the adjectives, although this fact is often obscured due to the tendency for the majority of adjectives to be one-place predicates.

2. Nominalization of Japanese adjectives

2.0. There are two morphological classes of adjectives in Japanese, often referred to as adjectives (A) and adjectival nouns (AN). Adjectives, ending with -i in the predicate position, inflect for tense and mood, while adjectival nouns take a copula: -na for the prenominal position, -da for the predicate position, and -ni for the adverbial form. We will not be concerned here about the difference of these two classes, since they behave in the same way under the particular derivations we will be discussing in this chapter. The term 'adjective' will henceforth be used to cover both classes.

We will first discuss two types of nominalization suffixes , one of which will be argued to be syntactic in our typology. Then, after reviewing the general problems associated with the argument structure and case marking of Japanese adjectives, we will use this syntactic suffixation as a test to clarify some issues.

2.1. Two types of nominalizing suffixes

In this section we will take up two nominalizing suffixes for Japanese adjectives and discuss their differences. The following are some examples of the adjectives that take both suffixes:

(15) takai 'high' taka-mi / taka-sa
 hukai 'deep' huka-mi / huka-sa
 akarui 'light' akaru-mi /akaru-sa
 omoi 'heavy' omo-mi / omo-sa
 tuyoi 'strong' tuyo-mi /tuyo-sa
 sinken 'serious' sinken-mi / sinken-sa

The suffix -mi attaches to about 30 adjectives, if we count the words that are commonly used, while the other suffix -sa seems to be completely productive. The basic semantic difference between the two forms is that A-sa denotes the abstract state or property while A-mi denotes a more concrete element bearing that property. The following examples illustrate this point:

(16) a. Kawa no huka-mi / *huka-sa ni hamat-ta.
      river GEN depth   LOC fall-PAST
      '(I) fell into the deep point of the river.'

   b. Kawa no *huka-mi / huka-sa ni odoroku.
      river GEN   depth   LOC be surprised
      '(I) am surprised by how deep the river is.'

(17) a. Yuka ga hon no omo-mi / *omo-sa de hekomu.
      floor NOM book GEN heavy-SUF   CAUSE dent
      'The floor got dented due to the weight of the books.'

   b. Hon no *omo-mi / omo-sa o hakaru.
      book GEN   weight ACC measure
      '(I) measure the weight of the books.'

Thus, while A-sa has a transparent meaning, the meaning of A-mi is not predictable. Roughly speaking, for huka-mi 'deep point', taka-mi 'high place' and so on, it denotes a particular point or place with that property; for yowa-mi 'a weakness', omo-mi '(heavy) weight', and so on, it denotes an entity with that property.

These observations lead us to believe that -mi suffixation should be part of the lexicon, while -sa is not. In the level-ordered morphology, that is, the former belongs to class 1 suffix while the latter to class 2 or higher.

This speculation is further confirmed by the fact that no adjectival compounds can feed the -mi suffixation while all of them can feed the -sa suffixation. See the following examples.

(17) hono-akarui --> hono-akaru-sa /*-mi (cf. akaru-mi)
     'slightly light'
     muzu-gayui --> muzu-gayu-sa /*-mi (cf. kayu-mi)
     'tickling and itchy'
     ama-zuppai --> ama-zuppa-sa /*-mi (cf. suppa-mi)
     'sweet and sour'
     soko-hukai --> soko-huka-sa /*-mi (cf. huka-mi)
     'bottom-deep, deep-bottomed'

Another property of the -sa suffixation that is not found with the -mi suffixation is that there exists a pattern of correspondence between S and the nominalization:

(18) X ga A. 'X is A.' --> X no A-sa 'X's A-ness'

This correspondence is especially clear when it is acting semantically as a clause nominalizer:

(19) Taroo wa Hanako no kasiko-sa ni kizuk-anai.
          TOP   GEN clever-ness LOC notice-NEG
     'Taro does not notice how clever Hanako is.'

On the other hand, some cases of the -mi suffixation cannot be accompanied by the genitive NP:

(20) a. hukami no aru midori 'deep green'
        depth GEN have green

     b. *midori no hukami 'green's depth'

We therefore conclude that these two nominalizing suffixes belong to different places in our typology. Namely, the -mi suffixation belongs to the lexical rule with morphological operation, while the -sa suffixation belongs to the syntactic rule with morphological operation. We will see further evidence below for the syntactic nature of the latter.

Kageyama (1982) has argued that -sa has the affix boundary (+), lower than the compound boundary (#i), or the phrasal boundary (#), given the facts that '-sa is attached to stems rather than full-fledged words and that it has no effect on the accentuation of whole derived words.' With this assumption he attempts to explain that a productive AN-forming SJ morpheme -teki (which has a compound boundary) cannot be nominalized with -sa, given the correctness of the level-ordering hypothesis.

(21) *genzitu-teki-sa 'realistic-ness'

*ippan-teki-sa 'general-ness'

This claim, however, creates more problems than it solves. First of all, it cannot explain why -sa can attach to compound adjectives, as shown in (17). Secondly, the fact that it does not affect the accent pattern can also follow from assigning it a phrasal boundary, which does not change the accent pattern either. As for the facts shown in (21) above, there is an alternative explanation that Kageyama himself suggests (and rejects). Namely, these examples are blocked by the existence of words with the SJ suffix -sei; gensitu-sei, ippan-sei, and so on.[3] In fact N-teki-sa

---

[3]For discussion of 'blocking' of a certain morphologically derived form by the existence of another form, see Aronoff (1976). In this particular case, even though N-teki-sa should be well-formed due to the productivity of -sa, the form N-sei is preferred over it,

becomes more acceptable when there is no corresponding form N-sei to that word honkaku-teki-sa / *honkaku-sei, contrary to the judgement reported by Kageyama (1982). We thus maintain that the -sa suffixation belongs to the syntactic rules.

2.2. Argument structure and case marking of adjectives

As is the case with English adjectives, a number of Japanese adjectives are one-place predicates. There are, however, a fair number of adjectives which occur with two NP's and they have been one source of a long-standing controversy in Japanese syntax, as we will see immediately below.

There are so-called 'stative predicates' in Japanese, which are characterized by taking the nominative (instead of accusative) case marking on their 'object' NP. Morphologically, many of them are adjectives, although a few verbs fall into this group as well. In terms of the case marking patterns, adjectives belonging to this class can be classified as follows:

(22) A. NP ni NP ga A. (ex. Boku ni kore ga omosiroi.)
         DAT   NOM   'I am amused at this.'

    B. NP ni/ga NP ga A. (Boku ni/ga hebi ga kowai.)
                           'I am fearful of snakes.'

    C. NP ga NP ga A. (Taroo ga turi ga umai.)
                           'Taro is good at fishing.'

---

probably because it is simpler in form, and also, since the stem is a SJ morpheme, a SJ suffix is preferred over a native one.

The difference between classes A and B above, namely whether a certain adjective allows the nominative as well as dative marker on the first NP is rather subtle. The basic controversy that surrounds these adjectives is as the following. One approach (e.g., Kuno, 1973) takes the nominative marker on the first NP to be basic (as the ordinary subject marker). The nominative marker on the second NP, on the other hand, is derived by the o/ga conversion, and the alternating dative marker on the first NP is derived by the ga/ni conversion. In short this approach derives these constructions with two-place adjectives from the ordinary transitive construction. The other approach takes the [NP ni NP ga A] as the basic pattern and derives the nominative marker on the first NP by a conversion rule. In this approach this construction is regarded as basically different from ordinary transitive constructions that take [NP ga NP o V]. Specifically, Kuroda (1978) has called this pattern 'ergative'. For the reasons to be discussed in this section, we will adopt the latter approach and call the constructions of (22 A, B) 'ergative'. ((22 C) will be discussed later.)

With these remarks on the particular problems associated with one class of adjectives, we can now list the basic classes of adjectives with their argument structure and case markings.

(23) A. Theme ga A. (ex. Yama ga takai.)
'Mountains are high.'

B. Exp. ga A. (ex. Boku ga uresii.)
'I am glad.'

C. Exp. ni Theme ga A. (Boku ni hebi ga kowai.)
'I am fearful of snakes.'

D. Theme ga Goal ni A. (Taroo ga Hanako ni yasasii.)
'Taro is kind to Hanako.'

E. Theme ga Obj. ni A. (Taroo ga samusa ni yowai.)
'Taro is weak against the cold.'

F. Theme ga [Theme ga A.] (Taroo ga se ga takai.)
'Taro is tall.'
(lit. T. is (height is tall).)

2.3. Complements under nominalization

We will examine in this section how the -sa suffixation applies to the adjectives that take more than one argument, and discuss what the result can tell us about the structure of sentences involving those adjectives.

Let us first see what happens with the nominalization of adjectives as classified in (23) above.

(24) A. Theme ga A. --> Theme no A-sa.
(Yama no taka-sa)

B. Exp. ga A. --> Exp. no A-sa.
(Boku no uresi-sa)

C. Exp. ni Theme ga A. --> (*Exp. no) Theme no A-sa
((*Boku no) hebi no kowa-sa)

D. Theme ga Goal ni A. --> Theme no (*Goal no) A-sa
(Taroo no (*Hanako no/ni) yasasi-sa)

E. Theme ga Obj. ni A. --> Theme no (*Obj. no) A-sa
(Taroo no (*samusa no/ni) yowa-sa)

F. Theme ga Theme ga A. --> Theme no Theme no A-sa
(Taroo no se no taka-sa)

The thematic function hierarchy for the genitive NP position in nominalization is the following: Theme > Experiencer > Oblique. We also note that the genitive NP most often corresponds to the nominative marked NP (but see below). As for the other complements of the adjectives, they cannot simply be inherited, as opposed to the cases we saw with English. One factor behind this difference is the restriction we have mentioned in the previous chapter that NP in Japanese cannot have a PP adjunct, but can only be modified by a genitive marked NP.

Now let us take a closer look at the 'ergative' adjectives mentioned above. Taking the classification of (22) above, the following illustrates the pattern of nominalization of these adjectives:

(25) A. NP ni NP ga A.
(*Boku no) eiga no omosiro-sa
'the movie's funniness (to me)'

(*Boku no) kodomo no kawai-sa
'the child's dear-ness (to me)'

B. NP ni/ga NP ga A.
(*Boku no) gan no osorosi-sa
'cancer's scariness (to me)'

(*Boku no) H. no urayamasi-sa
'H's envy-causing-ness (to me)'

(*Boku no) sore no hazukasi-sa
'its embarassing-ness (to me)'

(The class (22 C) will be discussed below.) We can see that the Experiencer argument can never realized as the genitive NP, even though many of them (i.e., those belonging to

(22B)) can take the nominative (instead of dative) marking. This fact indicates that the nominalization pattern does not correspond to the case markings. Note further that the situation in (25) above is in contrast with the nominalization of the ordinary transitive verbs, where both Agent and Patient can be realized by the genitive NP:

 (26) Ginkoo no doru no kaisime.
   bank GEN dollar GEN purchase
   'the purchase of the dollar by the bank'

The impossibility of nominalizing in this fashion on the part of the ergative adjectives here is significant, because this indicates that, at least in some respect, it is not plausible to treat these two-place adjectives on a par with the transitive verbs by manipulating just the surface case-markings (e.g., by o/ga and ga/ni conversions). Now observe the nominalization of the 'two-place' adjectives of (22) that cannot take the dative marking on the first NP. We notice that they fall into two groups; one that can take two genitive NP's and the other that cannot comfortably nominalize at all:

 (27) a. Taroo no tenisu no uma-sa /heta-sa
     GEN tennis GEN good bad
   'T's being good/bad at tennis'

  b. ??(Boku no) kuruma no hosi-sa / kai-ta-sa
     I GEN car GEN want buy-want
   'my wanting(to buy) a car.'

  c. *Boku no Hanako no suki-sa /kirai-sa
    I GEN   GEN like dislike
   'my (non-)fondness of Hanako'

There are several ways in which these adjectives are different from the ones shown in (26) and among themselves. First of all, they cannot omit the first NP without being elliptical. Secondly, the difference between (27a) and (27b,c) is that while the first NP in the latter is an Experiencer argument, the one in (27a) is a Theme argument. In other words adjectives of the class (22C) take two Theme arguments. This cannot be allowed under an ordinary conception of argument structure. On the other hand, everything seems to follow if we consider that these adjectives belong to the class (23F) above, namely that they make an A' with its immediate theme NP, which in turn takes another theme NP to make S, as shown below:

(28) a.
```
        S
       / \
      NP   A'
   Taroo ga / \
          NP   A
       Turi ga umai
```
b.
```
        N'
       / \
      NP   N'
   Taroo no / \
          NP   N
       Turi no / \
              A   sa
            uma-
```

Although the predicates such as <u>umai</u> 'good at' and <u>heta-da</u> 'bad at' are usually cited as predicates that take the nominative 'object' NP's (cf. Kuno 1973), it now seems more plausible to group them with those adjectives that form A' with its theme NP (class (23 F) above) as exemplified below, since they share the same nominalization pattern.

(29) a. Taroo ga asi ga hayai.
        NOM leg NOM fast 'T. runs fast.'
     Taroo no asi no haya-sa

b. Taroo ga zisin ga nai. 'T. lacks confidence.'
   NOM confidence NOM be(NEG)
   Taroo no zisin no na-sa

The examples in (29) can be naturally assigned the structures parallel to those shown in (28).

As for the unacceptability of (27b) and (27c), it will be argued in Chapter IV that those predicates are actually not two-place predicates, but the second NP is the object of the base verb from which the adjectival predicate is derived, as schematically shown below: (See Chapter IV for details.)

(30) a. Boku ga [kuruma o kai]-tai.

   b. Boku ga [kuruma ga [kai-tai]].

(31) a. Boku ga [Hanako o suk]-i da.

   b. Boku ga [Hanako ga [suki-da]].

Formally the predicate in (31) is not a genuine adjective, but is a derived noun. That is probably why these predicates (suki, kirai) cannot nominalize with this otherwise productive suffix -sa. They cannot combine with the verbalizing suffix -garu which is discussed in Section 3, either.

Thus the examination of the result of the nominalization makes clear that so-called 'two-place' (or 'object-ga' marking) adjectives actually fall into two groups:

(32) a. Ergative [Exp. ni/ga Theme ga A.]

   b. Double Theme [Theme ga [Theme ga A].]

We have seen that one of the difficulties in dealing with the (seemingly) two-place adjectives stems from the ambiguity in their case marking patterns. Namely, many of them can take the double nominative pattern when they are underlyingly different from each other. Although many problems surrounding them still remain, it was shown here that studying the patterns of the nominalization can contribute to the clarification of the following points. First, the difference between the nominalization of ordinary transitive predicates and the 'two-place' adjectives suggests that they are underlyingly different and one should not be derived from the other in terms of case marking conversion. Secondly, the nominalization test can isolate the 'double theme' adjectives among the 'two-place' adjectives. Thus, putting the class of desiderative adjectives aside (see Chapter IV), we can now state that 'two-place' adjectives are either ergative (NP ni/(ga) NP ga A.) or double theme (NP ga (NP ga A.).). This leaves us with no adjectives that must be assigned the double nominative case marking as the basic pattern. (See Chapter IV for more discussion.)

2.4. Extended domain of the nominalization

We will discuss in this section the interesting pattern on nominalization exhibited by predicates such as <u>hosii</u>, and V-<u>tai</u> in certain environments. Namely, when they are used to express strong desire, the nominalizing suffix can attach to a whole phrase, V'-tai/-i. See the following examples:

(33) a. Taroo wa [kane o hosi]-sa ni nusumi o sita.
　　　　　　TOP money ACC want CAUSE theft ACC do
　　　'Taro committed a robbery out of desire for money.'

b. Taroo wa [tesuto de ii ten o tori-ta]-sa no amari
　　　　TOP examLOC good markACC get-want GEN excess

　kanningu o sita.
　cunning ACC do

　'Taro cheated in the exam out of the desire to
　get good marks.'

c. Taroo wa [sono hon o te ni ire-ta]-sa no issin de
　　　　TOP that bookAC handLOCget-want GEM desire
　'Due to the strong desire to acquire that book,'

d. [Hanako ni ai-ta]-sa ga tunoru bakari da.
　　　　DATmeet want　NOM increase ever COP
　'my desire to meet H gets stronger and stronger.'

e. [anata ni home-rare-ta]-sa ni soo sita no desu.
　　　you DATpraise-PASS-want　CAUSE so do COP PART
　'I did it out of the desire to be praised by you.'

The significance of these examples is that they show almost any kind of V'-tai can be nominalized in these environments. So the phrases in the brackets above must be syntactically derived. Here we have another case of the phrasal suffixation construction. Note, however, that in these constructions -sa does not attach directly to a phrase, but rather it is the desiderative suffix -tai, that attaches to a V' and forms an A'.

These examples provide a strong piece of evidence for classifying the -sa suffixation as a syntactic rule with morphological operation. Kageyama (1982) also notes examples similar to (33 a,b), and states that we must admit a recursion from syntax to morphology for a small number of cases. Although his claim is in accordance with our contention, he states that such examples are confined to a fixed expression '-sa ni', and that we can constrain the (undesirable) recursion from syntax to morphology to the minimum by specifying these fixed expressions. As we have seen by (33), the environment of this type of phrasal suffixation cannot quite be limited to one or two specific expressions. Instead of allowing a limited recursion from syntax to morphology, we have designated certain processes of morphology with complete transparency and productivity to be part of syntax, and allowed the interaction of phrasal and morphological operations there.

Our conjecture that these cases of phrasal suffixation are possible because of the productivity of both the V' suffix and the nominalization suffix is further confirmed by the existence of another construction of similar properties; this time with the 'tough' predicates, -yasui 'easy to' -nikui 'hard to', and their nominalization.

There is no space here to discuss the details of 'tough' constructions in Japanese, but let us just note that there are two kinds of 'tough' constructions; the one that involves a relation-changing (34a) and the one that does not (34b). (See Inoue 1978 for details.) In both cases the adjectival 'tough' suffixes attach to the infinitive form of the verb:

(34) a. Taroo ga damasi-yasui. 'T. is easy to deceive.'
      NOM deceive-easy

b. Taroo ga damas-are-yasui.
   NOM deceive-PASS-easy
   'Taro tends to be deceived (easily).'

Both types of 'tough'-predicates readily nominalize with their subject NP in the genitive NP:

(35) a. Taroo no damasi-yasu-sa

b. Taroo no damas-are-yasu-sa

This 'tough'-suffixation is a completely productive and transparent process, and it is natural to classify it as a syntactic process with morphological operation. Thus the fact that the nominalization can operate on the 'tough' predicates is another indication for the syntactic nature of this nominalization.

(35ab) provide a contrast with the equivalent English constructions as the following, to which we will divert for some remarks.

(36) a. John is easy to deceive.

b. *John's easiness to deceive.

(37) a. John tends to be deceived (easily).

b. John's tendency to be deceived (easily).

Examples such as (36b) have been used to argue for the existence of the 'tough' movement in English. Namely, if 'John' in (36a) is not the 'deep subject' of the sentence, (36b) can be blocked with the assumption that the nominalization does not apply to the structure after the movement has applied, which accounts for the contrast between (36b) and the following:

(38) a. John is eager to succeed.

b. John's eagerness to succeed.

On the other hand, consider (37b) above. It is also the case that 'John' is not the 'deep subject' in (37a), but (37b) is grammatical. (Also consider: John's certainty to win.) In this connection it was mentioned in Chapter II that there exists a contrast between sentences like (36a) and (38a) in that the former can form a complex adjective ('easy-to-please person') while the latter cannot ('*eager-to-please person'). This contrast was accounted for by the generic condition of word formation in general, based on the observation that the subject of the infinitival subject in (36a) is an arbitrary PRO while the one in (38a) is a controlled PRO. This difference seems to be also responsible for the contrast we find in the nominalization pattern here. Note that while (36a) has an arbitrary PRO in the infinitive, both (37a) and (37b) have a controlled PRO. Note further the ungrammaticality of the nominalization of 'object deletion' adjectives that also have an arbitrary PRO as the infinitival subject:

(39) a. The meal is ready to serve.
    b. *the meal's readiness to serve
       (cf. John's readiness to leave)

(40) a. Mary is pretty to look at.
    b. *Mary's prettiness to look at

These observations lead us to the following conjecture. One condition on complement inheritance under nominalization is that the subject of the infinitival complement must be controlled by the subject of the nominalization. We might give the intuitive motivation for this condition as follows: complement inheritance requires the path of control to be just one; namely, the genitive NP (as the subject) controls both the nominalized predicate and the infinitival complement. Hence this 'path of control' cannot be blocked by PRO that is not subject-controlled, as in the cases of (36), (39), and (40).

Actually, this condition might be looked at as a more general condition on the lexical rule that involves complement inheritance. Consider the well-known Visser's generalization pair:

(41) a. *John was promised [PRO to leave].

b. John$_i$ was persuaded [PRO$_i$ to leave].

c. John's$_i$ promise [PRO$_i$ to leave].

Note that the PRO in (41a) is not controlled by the subject of the higher verb while the one in (41b) is. If we consider the passive operation to be applying on the VP with an infinitival complement (cf. Keenan 1980 for arguments), we can look at (41) as another instance of complement inheritance that obeys the same condition. Note that (41c) is grammatical, where the condition is met for 'promise' under nominalization. In regard to this point just mentioned, compare (41a) with the following, which appear to be counterexamples to our hypothesis.

(42) a. [The city was destroyed] to prove a point.

b. [The city's destruction] to prove a point.

Such examples have been given (cf. Roeper 1983) to show the existence of an implicit agent argument (presumably a PRO) in these constructions, on the assumption that the purpose clause must have a controller. We see that these sentences are grammatical despite the presence of the non-subject-controlled (i.e., by-Agent controlled) infinitive. Note, however, that in (42) the purpose clauses are sister not to the V or N but to S or NP as a modifier of some sort.⁴ (See the bracketing in (42).) Thus (42a,b) are not actually counterexamples but they show that the condition we propose here concerns only the infinitival complement that is preserved under morphological derivations, namely, those that occur as sister to the derived V or N. We consequently maintain that there exists a condition on the morphological operation on V or A with an infinitival complement that its PRO must be controlled by the subject of the derived head element.

---

⁴Note that clefting the to-VP in the cases we have consedered above yields ungrammatical sentences as opposed to (42).
  i. *It is to succeed that John is eager.
 ii. *It is to please that John is easy.
iii. *It is to leave that John was persuaded.
(cf. It is to prove a point that the city was destroyed.)

We have observed here that among various [A to VP] constructions, the ones that can form a lexical unit of complex adjectives (easy-to-please, ready-to-serve) and the ones that can nominalize with their complement (eagerness to please) show a complementary distribution, and that the salient difference between them is the nature of PRO subject that they have; PROarb for the former, controlled PRO for the latter. Note that it follows from our general framework that the lexical unit formation applies only to the former type of adjective phrase, and the nominalization to the latter. The lexical unit formation, which forms a complex adjective, is a lexical rule fed by phrasal operation (class B) in our typology. It forms a complex word (e.g., easy-to-please) out of a sequence of words in the surface structure ([easy PRO to please t]). Since the output is a 'word', it must obey the generic condition that governs words in general (see Chapter II, Section 1.5.), and that is why the PRO in the input construction must be arbitrary. On the other hand, the case of complement inheritance such as eagerness to please is a regular word formation (eager+ness) with the subcategorized complement preserved and realized in syntax. Note that the output is not a complex word, but is an ordinary phrase that obeys the PSR. It then follows that the control relation between the infinitival subject PRO and the subject of the adjective should also hold in the derived construction. In fact we now have a reason to assume that only subject-controlled PRO (as opposed to arbitrary PRO, Agent-controlled PRO) is allowed in this type of construction. The proposed condition is quite likely due to the problem of parsing, as suggested above that the 'path of control' cannot be blocked in a morphologically derived construction. Thus our rule typology can account for the different conditions that the two processes (lexical unit formation / the complement inheritance) that we have considered here impose on their input structure.

Now we leave this diversion and go back to the nominalization of Japanese 'tough' predicates. Here there is no infinitival phrase involved, (cf. (35a,b)) but just a derived adjective of the form V-suff(A). Consequently, there is no restriction on the way they can nominalize, as opposed to the cases in English we have just discussed. Rather, what is significant here is the fact that the 'tough' suffix (especially of the type (34b)) sometimes attaches to V', and that it provides another environment where -sa can attach to a unit larger than a word. In other words, although -sa by itself cannot attach to a phrase in general, as we have seen with various 'two-place' adjectives above, its complete productivity forces it to attach not only to simple adjectives but also to V'+suff.(A) construction. We find the following sort of examples to be acceptable:

(43) a. Nihonzin no ryuukoo ni/*no sayuu-s-are-yasu-sa o
       Japanese GEN fashion DAT/GEN move doPASS easy   ACC

```
        hihan-suru-na.
        criticize-NEG. IMPERA
```

   'Don't criticize the tendency of the Japanese
   to be affected easily by fashion.'

b. Kono shu no topikku no nyuusu ni nari-niku-sa
   this kind GEN topic GEN news COP become-hard
   'The difficulty of this sort of topic's being
    made into a news item.'

c. Kono yakuhin no mizu to maziri-niku-sa o
   this chemical GEN water with mix   hard

   zikken ni riyoo suru.
   experiment LOC use

   'In the experiment we make use of this
   chemical's tendency to not mix with water.'

The fact that there exists such examples of -sa nominalization in turn confirms the assumption that an adjectival suffix such as -yasui, -nikui attach to a V'.

3. On the verbalizing suffix -garu

In this section we will examine a verbalizing suffix that productively attaches to a certain class of adjectives in Japanese. As it was found with the nominalizing suffix, we will find that this suffix is also sensitive to the argument structure of adjectives, and it attaches to a phrasal suffix -tai in the predicted manner.

Morphologically, the suffix -garu changes an adjective into a verb. In its semantic function -garu turns an 'internal feeling' predicate into an ordinary predicate with the meaning 'showing the feeling x.' It has long been noted that so-called 'psychological predicates' in Japanese cannot occur with the third person subject NP in the neutral style,

(44) a. ??Taroo ga samui. 'T. is cold.'

b. ??Taroo ga kanasii. 'T. is sad.'

and that the suffix -garu must be attached to these predicates to make the sentence sound natural.

(45) a. Taroo ga samu-gat-te iru. (progressive form)

b. Taroo ga kanasi-gat-te iru.

It is in this context that this particular suffix has been mainly discussed in the literature, but its properties have otherwise not been discussed in much detail (but see below).

One formal account of -garu appears in Abe (1981b). He analyzes it as a transitivizer, converting a one-place adjective into a two-place verb.

(46) a. (Taroo ni) eiga ga omosiroi.
   DAT movie NOM fun
   'Movies are fun for Taro.'

b. Taroo ga eiga o omosiro-garu.

In Abe's (1981b) framework of categorial grammar, there is no notion of 'ergative' predicates, so an adjective like omosiroi is a one-place predicate. Thus there seems to be no principled reason in his analysis why it is the Experiencer NP of the adjective that fills the subject position in (46b). Furthermore, as we have already seen by the examples in (45) above, -garu also attaches to a genuine one-place adjective like samui 'cold', and derives an intransitive verb samu-garu 'show the feeling of being cold'. It is immediately clear then that -garu cannot simply be described as a transitivizer, and that it is not possible to capture its behavior solely by the notion of transitivity. Rather, what we should note is the fact that -garu always takes the Experiencer argument of an adjective as the subject. See the following illustration of this point.

(47) a. Exp. ga A. --> Exp. ga A-garu.

(Taroo ga uresi-garu. 'Taro acts happy.'

b. Theme ga A. --> Exp. ga Theme o A-garu.

(Taroo ga hon o omota-garu.

'Taro finds the book heavy.')

c. Exp.ni Th. ga A. --> Exp. ga Th o A-garu.

(Taroo ga hebi o kowa-garu. 'T. fears snakes.')

We can say that -garu converts a basically ergative case pattern of adjectives (of feelings) into a transitive case pattern typical of verbs. The claim that the suffixation of -garu is sensitive to the argument structure of adjectives is further supported by the fact that if a one-place Theme adjective is not capable of optionally taking an Experiencer argument, this suffixation does not apply. In semantic terms this means that adjectives that can occur with -garu denote a property that belongs to the subjective feelings. For instance, it seems that color terms can never occur with -garu. (cf. *aka'red'-garu, *siro'white'-garu, etc.)

As noted in Abe (1981b), -garu can attach to various derived adjectives. For instance, there are some fairly productive A/V conversion patterns as exemplified below:

(48) a. V-asi --> A

urayam / urayam-asii 'envious'

wazurau / wazur-asii 'bothersome'

b. A-mu --> V

osii / osi-mu 'to miss'

tanosii / tanosi-mu 'enjoy'

The suffix -garu can attach to these adjectives and add to this pattern of conversion.

(49) a. NP ga NP o urayamu. 'NP envies NP.'

NP ni NP ga urayam-asii.

NP ga NP o urayam-asi-garu.

b. NP ni NP ga osii. 'NP misses NP.'

NP ga NP o osi-mu.

NP ga NP o osi-garu.

Further, it has been noted by many (e.g., Kuno 1973) that -garu attaches to the desiderative suffix -tai and it cancels the 'object-ga' marking induced by -tai:

(50) a. Taroo ga [mizu o nomi]-tai.

'T. wants to drink water.'

b. Taroo ga mizu ga nomi-tai.

c. Taroo ga mizu o nomi-ta-garu.

This fact has been accounted for (e.g., Kageyama 1982) by the percolation of the feature [+stative] of the head element, which triggers the 'object-ga' marking.

(51) a.   [+stative]   b. [-stative]

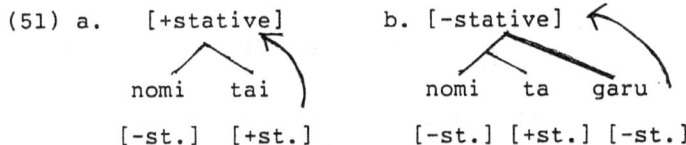

    nomi tai   nomi ta garu

    [-st.] [+st.]   [-st.] [+st.] [-st.]

In this view the case markings of (50a-c) are determined solely by the category of V under which the suffixations are performed. On the other hand, we have already seen some evidence from the way V'-tai are nominalized with -sa that the desiderative suffix -tai basically attaches to the category of V'. (This position will be argued for in its full details in Chapter IV.) If we maintain that assumption (as the bracketing of (50a) shows), and also that -garu attaches to that constituent, then we would predict that despite its appearance (50c) is not a truly transitive construction but rather an intransitive construction:

(50)c' Taroo ga [[mizu o nomi]-ta]-garu.

This prediction is borne out, as demonstrated by the fact that sentences of the form (50.c) cannot passivize:[5]

(52) a. Taroo wa Hanako o sasoi-ta-gat-te iru.
'Taro wants to ask Hanako out.'

b. *Hanako wa Taroo ni sasoi-ta-gar-are-te iru.

Compare (52) with the following, which involves the predicate with the morphologically similar derivational history (V->A->V).

(53) a. Taroo wa Hanako o urayam-asi-gat-te iru.

'Taro envies Hanako.'

b. Hanako wa Taroo ni urayam-asi-gar-are-te iru.

---

[5]This does not, of couse, preclude the possibility of adversative passivization, which can apply to intransitive verbs.
(i) Taroo wa kodomo ni iede-si-ta-gar-are te komatta.
    TOP child DAT run away want PASS   troubled
'T. is troubled because his child wants to run away.'

The derivation of the predicate in (53), however, does not involve a V' category, so (53a) is a transitive construction as the possibility of passivization shows. This contrast is significant, especially in view of the lexicalist analysis proposed for the suffixation in (52) and (53), which cannot distinguish them in any principled way.

Note that the standard transformational analysis (cf. Kuno 1973) with sentence embedding, EQUI, and verb raising at the end of the cycle cannot naturally account for the unacceptability of (52b). It is because when -garu attaches to the verb by verb raising in the last cycle, [NP o V] is not a constituent any more due to the verb raising in the previous cycle:[6]

(54) a. [T ga [T ga [T ga H o sasoi]-ta]-garu.

b. [T ga [T ga H o sasoi-ta]-garu.

This concludes the discussion of -garu. We argued that this suffix is not a transitivizing suffix but rather what it does is convert the ergative pattern into the transitive pattern. It also requires the Experiencer argument to be the subject NP of the derived verb, and hence is sensitive to the argument structure of the adjectives it attaches to. Further, we have demonstrated that -garu attaches to the

---

[6] In order to block such ungrammatical sentences as (52b) Kuno (1978) assumes a Global Constraint, originally attributed to Harada, which prohibits the Passive from subjectivizing an NP that used to be a constituent of a sentence embedded in the sentence to which the rule applies.

V'-tai constituent. We will argue in the following chapter for the status of -tai as a phrasal suffix and discuss the consequences of that claim.

CHAPTER IV

PHRASAL SUFFIXES I: ALTERNATING CASE MARKING

In this chapter we will take up some stative predicates in Japanese which allow so-called 'object- ga marking', and argue that various facts about them can be better explained if we assume that some suffixes are 'flexible' in their subcategorization in that they basically attach to V' category but sometimes are best analyzed as attaching only to the verb of V' as a result of reanalysis on the surface constituents. The particular form of the reanalysis that we are concerned with here is as the following:

(1) a. [X V]v! + suff. ---> b. [X] [V + suff.]

1. Phrasal suffixation and reanalysis

In the framework assumed here suffixation to a phrase is perceived as a syntactic rule with morphological operation; in this case, a phrase of a category V' is formed by a rule of type A (syntactic rule by syntactic operation--see Chapter I for the rule typology), then the output is fed to a rule of type B (syntactic rule with morphological operation). As is the property of syntactic rules, the process (1a) above is regular, not constrained in terms of idiosyncracies (see below for examples). As it was briefly mentioned in Chapter I, phrasal suffixation can potentially build a structure that is not derived by phrase structure rules. Suppose the suffix has the feature [+N] and the verb subcategorizes for a direct object NP.

(2) [NP-o V]v' + suff.(N) ---> [NP-o [V + suff.]N]

Such a sequence, a nominal predicate follwing an accusative NP is not generated by PSRs of Japanese but only by this type of special suffixation. (See Chapter V for the discussion of this particular type of suffixation.) A similar case from Greenlandic Eskimo is reported by Sadock (1980). In Greenlandic noun incorporation, morphemes can incorporate a possessed NP, which is a syntactic phrase:

(3) [NP-erg. N] + verb ---> [NP-erg.] [N-verb]

Since a possessive NP gets an ergative case, the resulting sequence of an ergative NP followed by an intransitive verb is not observed in Greenlandic other than in this type of noun incorporation. Sadock (1980) points out that this property of being able to build a new structure is, according to Wasow's (1977) criteria, that of syntactic rules rather than lexical rules.

It can consequently be said that certain cases of syntactic word formation rule create a 'marked' structure in the language. It is also conceivable that this type of structure building can result in a structural ambiguity, which is often susceptible to a reanalysis. For instance, suppose a verb of a category X assigned a certain case x for its object argument, while a verb of a category Y assigned a different case y, and there existed a V'-suffix with the feature [+V, +Y], which can attach to a verb of a category X:

(4) [NP-x V[+X]] + suff.[+V,+Y]

This suffixation results in a marked structure in the language; namely, an NP of case x followed by a verb of a category Y:

(5) NP-x V-suff.[+Y]

It is conceivable that the NP in (5) get reanalyzed as an argument of the complex verb as a whole and assigned a case y instead:

(6) NP-y [V-suff.[+Y]]

by analogy to a more unmarked construction in the language.

2. Facts about Japanese stative predicate constructions

It is well known that the predicates in Japanese with the feature [+stative] assign a nominative case <u>ga</u> to their 'object NP' (henceforth 'second NP)[1] Also, many of them can mark their subject NP with dative case as well as nominative case. Semantically these are predicates expressing feelings, desire, non-intentional perception, ability, and so on. Morphologically they can be verb, adjective, or adjectival nouns:

---

[1] See Section 6 for discussion on why we do not want to refer to them as 'object'.

(7) Taroo ga/ni hebi ga kowai. (adjective)
    NOM/DAT snake NOM fearful
    'Taro is fearful of snakes.'

(8) Taroo ga/ni eigo ga dekiru. (verb)
    NOM/DAT Eng.NOM can do
    'Taro can speak English.'

(9) Taroo ga/*ni Hanako ga suki-da. (adj. noun)
    NOM/DAT   NOM like COP.
    'Taro likes Hanako.'

It is also the case that verbs suffixed with a desiderative suffix $\underline{-tai}$ and potential $\underline{-(r)eru}$ mark their second NP with $\underline{ga}$:

(10) Taroo ga/ni eigo ga hanas-eru.
     NOM/DAT Eng.NOM speak-can
     'Taro can speak English.'

(11) Taroo ga/*ni eigo ga hanasi-tai.
     NOM/DAT Eng.NOM speak-want
     'Taro wants to speak English.'

The standard analysis for sentences like (7)-(11) is to assume certain predicates to bear the feature [+stative] lexically assigned to them and trigger a case marking conversion of $\underline{o}$ --> $\underline{ga}$ on the 'object' NP. (See Kuno 1973.) When the [+stative] predicate is a 'higher' predicate as in (10) and (11), this conversion takes place on the higher cycle:

(12) a. [Taroo ga eigo o hanasi]

   b. [Taroo ga [Taroo ga eigo o hanasi] -tai]
              ↓   ↓
              ∅   ga

   c. Taroo ga eigo ga hanasi-tai.

In some cases this conversion is followed by an optional conversion of ga --> ni on the subject NP. As shown above some predicates (cf. 9, 11) do not allow this dative case on the subject NP, which presumably has to be marked on the predicate as its idiosyncratic feature.

It has been noted that under certain circumstances there is an alternative set of case markings as shown below:

(13) Taroo ga eigo o hanas-eru.

(14) Taroo ga eigo o hanasi-tai.

In the accounts given so far, this fact can be dealt with by somehow preventing the feature [+stative] from becoming a feature of the whole predicate, so that the o --> ga conversion is blocked. For instance, Kageyama (1982) suggests that feature percolation must be blocked in the following structure in order for the alternating case marking pattern to be allowed.

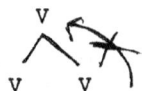

-tai [+stative]

The ga --> ni conversion on the subject NP does not take place if the object is marked with o:

(15) *Taroo ni eigo o hanas-eru (koto).

The ungrammaticality of a sentence like (15) has been accounted for by postulating the general principle that every sentence must have a nominative NP. (See Shibatani 1978.)

3. Proposal

Although the account given is sufficient to generate both (11)-(12) and (13)-(14), it does not predict when we get one form rather than the other at all. As we will see below, the two sets of case markings of (11)-(12) and (13)-(14) are not interchangeable in many instances. The preference of one pattern over the other with this construction is sometimes rather subtle and also seems to vary with different speakers. Nevertheless, there seem to be several factors that are relevant in the choice of one pattern over the other.

What we will do in the following is to propose that this alternating case marking is due to the reanalysis of a V'-suffix as a V-suffix under certain circumstances. It will be argued that many of the factors that seem to be relevant here fall together if we consider them as part of the environment for this reanalysis.

Using the sentences (11)-(14), we will now illustrate our hypothesis. First, we assume that the suffixes -tai and -reru basically subcategorize for a V'. In the traditional transformational approach to these constructions they are supposed to have the following underlying structures, with the suffixes being the sister to an S node.

(16) a. 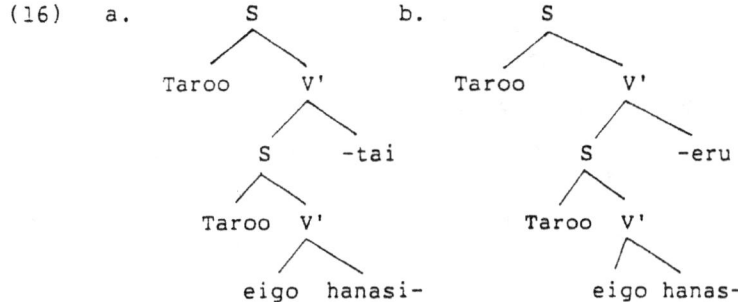 b.

However, when the suffixation takes place as a result of the predicate raising on the higher cycle, the suffixes are actually sister to V', not S. This is because both -tai and -reru are so-called 'Equi' predicates, which require the subject NP's in both S's to be coreferential. So the relevant structure when the suffixation takes place is the following:[2]

(17) a. 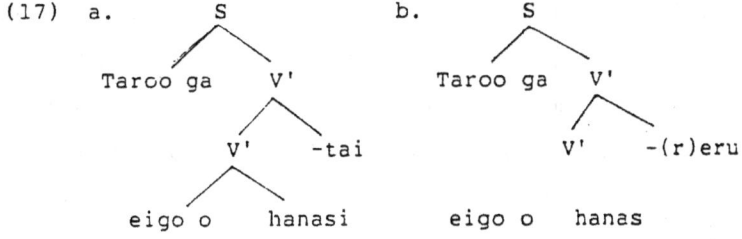 b.

The assumption that -tai and -reru attach to V' is supported by the fact that they can attach to conjoined V''s:

---

[2] The mapping of (16) to (17) can presumably be accounted for by 'rules of LF' rather than by syntactic transformations, but the discussion here holds equally well for that approach.

(18) Taroo wa [gakkoo e itte, tomodati ni ai]-tai/-eru.
     TOP school GOAL go   friends DAT see
  'Taro wants to/can go to school and see friends.'

but not to conjoined S's with different subject NP's:

(19) [Taroo wa utai, Hanako wa odori]-tai/-eru.
     --->*Taroo wa utai, Hanako wa odori-tai/odor-eru.
         TOPsing   TOP dance
  'Taro wants to sing, and Hanako wants to dance.'
  'Taro can sing, and Hanako can sing.'

This assumption about V' suffixation seems to be also natural when we consider the semantic scope of these suffixes.

Going back now to (17), after the suffixation takes place we get the following set of strings:

(20) a. [[eigo o hanasi]-tai]

     b. [[eigo o hanas]-eru]

Since -tai is lexically an adjective the result is an adjective preceded by an accusative NP, which does not conform to any phrase structure rules of Japanese. There is no adjective that subcategorizes for an accusative NP. This is an instance of structure building discussed in Section 1 above, which, according to our assumption on syntactic word formation, occurs only with phrasal affixation. Similarly, although the suffix -reru is lexically a verb, it is marked [+stative], and there is no simple verb with that feature which subcategorizes for an accusative NP in Japanese. (See below for the discussion of apparent counterexamples.) As discussed in Section 2, all simple [+stative] predicates in Japanese mark their second NP with ga.

It is now easy to see that the environment for reanalysis is supplied in (20a,b). All that is needed is rebracketing:

(21) a. Taroo ga [eigo ga [hanasi-tai]]

   b. Taroo ga [eigo ga [hanas-eru]]

The NP is interpreted as an argument of the stative predicate as a whole, and hence is assigned the nominative case marking.

Our hypothesis is, then, that the case marking of sentences (11)-(12) is a result of reanalysis based on (13)-(14). We will now see what kinds of predictions this hypothesis can actually lead us to.

4. Morphological transparency

Our hypothesis immediately predicts that in order for the alternating case marking patterns to exist for one predicate, the predicate must be morphologically complex in order for the base for reanalysis to exist. It is briefly noted in Kuno(1973: 95) that the alternating case marking exists only with 'stative derivatives', by which Kuno refers to complex predicates involving -tai and -reru. Our hypothesis naturally predicts that. Besides -tai and -reru predicates, however, there exist a few stative predicates which can occasionally take accusative NP's which nevertheless are not generally considered as derivatives. These predicates are suki-da, kirai-da, hosii, and wakaru.

We will take up the first three predicates first, which are given in the following examples:

(22) Taroo wa Hanako ga/o suki-da/kirai-da.
     TOP   NOM ACC like dislike
    'Taro likes/dislikes Hanako.'

(23) Boku wa konna kuruma ga/o hosii.
      I TOP such car   NOM ACC want
    'I want a car like this one.'

Even though these constructions are not generally considered as involving a higher predicate, these predicates are nonetheless morphologically related to corresponding verbs which mark their second NP with an accusative case. They are shown below:

(24) Taroo wa Hanako o suku/kirau.
    'Taro likes/dislikes Hanako.'

(25) Boku wa kono kuruma o hossuru.
    'I want this car.'

It is then possible to say that when the second NP is marked with a nominative case, it is an instance of reanalysis parallel to the cases with -tai and -reru:

(26) Taroo ga [Hanako o suk] -i-da. --->
     Taroo ga [Hanako ga [suki-da]].

(27) Boku ga [kono kuruma o hos] -ii. --->
     Boku ga [kono kuruma ga [hosii]].

One difference between these cases and the ones involving higher predicates is that with (26) and (27) a nominative marking on the second NP is preferred to an accusative marking in most contexts. So it might be considered that with these predicates the reanalyzed form is the unmarked form. Note that the morphological derivation we have here is not productive at all³ like the suffixation of -tai and -reru. Hence it is easier for these forms to be lexicalized with the reanalyzed case pattern. (See Section 6 for further discussion and theoretical implications.)

There is an additional small piece of evidence showing that morphological transparency affects the reanalysis. Observe the following examples:

(28) a. Boku wa Hanako ga/o suki-da.
'I like Hanako.'

b. Boku wa Hanako ga/??o dai-suki-da.
'I like Hanako very much.'

The emphatic prefix dai- attaches only to [+N] category. So the prefixation of dai- strengthens the adjectival nominal interpretation of the predicate suki and makes the morphological relation to the verb less transparent. The less acceptable status of the accusative marking in (28b) can be attributed to this morphological difference between

---

³Besides the ones discussed above, there is one expression o-ki-ni-iri (A) 'favorite' derived from the verb expression ki ni iru (lit. 'suit one's feeling'): Tanaka-sensei wa Hanako ga/o o-ki-ni-iri da 'Hanako is Prof. T's favorite'. This expression is lexicalized and must be used with this honorific prefix, o-. Thus, generally speaking, although the nominal formation from a verb stem by adding -i is extremely common, it rarely forms an adjectival nominal. For example, from a verb nozomu 'to hope for' a noun nozomi 'a hope' can be derived, while an adjective nozomi (what would be a parallel form to suki) does not exist. On the other hand, the derivation of hosii (Adj) from hossuru (V) is idiosyncratic in form, while a parallel derivation with a suffix -asii is semi-productive; ex. nozom-asii 'desirable'. This suffix, however, does not allow the case alternation as we discuss here; sore ga/*o nozomasii 'that is desirable'. Thus this affix attaches only to V, but not to V'. For discussion of this suffix and others relating adjective and verb, see Chapter III.

the two predicates.

We should now consider the exceptional nature of the predicate wakaru, which can be preceded by both o-marked NP and ga-marked NP:

(29) a. Boku ga/ni kimi no kimoti ga wakaru.
       I NOM/DAT you POSS feelings NOM understand.
    b. Boku ga kimi no kimoti o wakaru (koto).
       'I understand your feelings.'

This predicate cannot be given a parallel analysis, since it is a lexical verb and not a derivative in any sense. Although wakaru has been treated as a stative predicate, it has been a problem for many analyses because it can occur in an imperative mood or with V-oo-to-suru, ('try to V'), which should be incompatible with stative predicates:

(30) a. Boku no kimoti o/*ga wakare (to wa iwanai).
       I POSS feelingsACC/NOMunderstand (not say)
       ' (I'm not telling you to) understand my feelings.'

    b. Kimi wa boku no kimoti o/*ga wakar-oo-to-si-nai.
       you TOP I POSS feelings ACC/NOM understand-try-not
       'You don't try to understand my feelings.'

Note that in (30) the nominative marking in place of the accusative marking is not possible.

These facts about wakaru can be accounted for rather straightforwardly if we postulate that there are two wakaru's one [+stative] and the other [-stative]. Stative wakaru, like any other simple stative predicates, takes dative or nominative for the first NP and nominative for the second NP. The non-stative one, like any other non-stative predicate, takes nominative for the first NP and accusative for the second NP, and can occur with imperative mood or -oo-to-suru.

5. Conditions for the reanalysis

Of the putative cases involving the type of reanalysis we are postulating for stative predicates, the cases with the predicates suffixed with -tai seem to be most actively used. We will see below that a number of conditions for the alternating case marking can be best understood as conditions for reanalysis. It is hard to show that parallel conditions exist for -reru also. It is conceivable that this is due to the fact that a sentence with -reru can have an ergative case pattern as well as accusative and double nominative ones. (See Section 6 for the discussion.) We will only note in this section for V-reru that semantic factors do affect whether the reanalyzed structure is preferred or not.

5.1. Distance between the second NP and the predicate

There is a general tendency with -tai constructions that double nominative marking occurs most naturally if the second NP is placed immediately preceding the predicate, whereas it is less acceptable if there is a constituent intervening between the second NP and the predicate. This is illustrated by the following examples:

(31) a. Boku wa nekkorogatte terebi ga mi-tai.
     I TOP lying down   TV   NOM watch-want
'I want to watch TV, lying down.'

b.??Boku wa terebi ga nekkorogatte mi-tai.

c. Boku wa terebi o nekkorogatte mi-tai.

The contrast between (31a-c) follows from our proposal. Since the reanalysis we are stipulating is done on the surface constituent of [NP V]-tai, in order for the NP to be interpreted as the argument of the reanalyzed predicate [V-tai], the NP must be interpreted as sister to the predicate. In other words, the reanalysis is a local process, and we will see more evidence for this point below. A similar situation holds with the sentences where both a direct object and an indirect object are present:

(32) a. Boku wa Hanako ni purezento o age-tai.
     I TOP Hanako DAT presentACC give-want
'I want to give a present to Hanako.'

b. Boku wa purezento o Hanako ni age-tai.

c. Boku wa Hanako ni purezento ga age-tai.

d.?Boku wa purezento ga Hanako ni age-tai.

Again, it is rather awkward for the dative NP, an argument of the verb alone and not V + suffix, to separate the nominative NP and the predicate, as shown in (32d).

This fact about the distance between the NP and the predicate has been noted by others (Shibatani 1979, Yoshida 1971, etc.). When we look at more data, however, we notice that it is not only the distance that actually matters. See the following example:

(33) Boku wa terebi ga totemo mi-tai.
    I TOP TV NOM very see-want
'I want to watch TV very much.'

The crucial difference between (31b) and (33) is the fact that the intervening constituent in (31b) is an adverbial modifying the verb _miru_ only, while the degree expression _totemo_ in (33) modifies _mitai_ as a whole. Hence, the adverbial in (33) is consistent with the interpretation of the suffixed predicate as a whole and the preceding NP as sister to it. The adverbial in (31b), on the other hand, contributes to separate the verb and the suffix by modifying just the verb. Thus the distance condition seems to boil down to the following: the predicate and the second NP cannot be separated by an argument or a modifier of the verb alone. In other words, the reanalysis can involve only the predicate and the second NP. The fact that those other elements can occur preceding the second NP even when it is nominative shows the locality of the reanalysis.

What is significant about this condition is that while it can be perceived naturally as a condition on the reanalysis, it cannot be easily accounted for otherwise; especially in the previous analysis with the feature [+stative] on the predicate, the feature percolation of the suffix to the predicate as a whole cannot be conditioned by the surface word order.

5.2. Conjunction and comparatives

We have mentioned above that _-tai_ can attach to conjoined V''s (cf. (18) and below). If our hypothesis is correct, it predicts that conjoined V''s cannot have the second NP marked with a nominative case, since [NP ga V] is not a constituent under the reanalyzed surface structure. On the other hand, an accusative-marked NP (or any other oblique-marked NP) and a verb is a V' constituent. This prediction is borne out.

(34) a.*Boku wa [koocha ga nomi, keeki ga tabe]-tai.
       I TOP   tea NOM drink cake NOM eat   want
    'I want to drink tea and eat cake.'

b. Boku wa [koocha o nomi, keeki o tabe]-tai.

c. Boku wa koocha ga nomi-tai-shi, keeki ga tabe-tai.

Note that this fact also cannot be accounted for using the feature on the predicate. By the time conjunction reduction applies, the case marking on the second NP has already been changed. As shown by (34c), however, nominative marking on the second NP is grammatical if the conjunction includes the suffix as well; so there is no way of blocking (34a), while generating (34b), in the previous analysis. A similar problem would arise in an approach (such as GPSG) where conjunction of deep structure constituents is postulated; assuming -tai subcategorizes for V' and bears a feature [+stative], which, via percolation to V, can trigger a nominative marking on the NP (by metarule), there seems to be no non-ad hoc way of preventing the feature percolation in case V' consists of conjoined V''s as in (34b).

The distance condition discussed in the preceding section allows the latter object NP of (34b) to be interpreted as the argument of [V-tai], and the following sentence is acceptable; marginal to some speakers, but definitely better than (34a):

(34) d. Boku wa koocha o nomi, keeki ga tabe-tai.

This, again, shows that the reanalysis of the predicate is local and not across-the-board.

Similarly, comparative constructions such as the following support our proposal:

(35) a. Boku, koohii yori biiru ga nomi-tai.
       I   cofee than beer NOM drink-want
   'I want to drink beer rather than cofee.'

   b. Boku, biiru ga koohii yori nomi-tai.

(36) a. Boku, koohii yori biiru o nomi-tai.

   b.*?Boku, biiru o koohii yori nomi-tai.

To my knowledge there has been no explicit analysis of such comparative constructions in Japanese. It is nevertheless plausible to think that (35a)/(36a) are more basic than (35b)/(36b) respectively,⁴ and that (35a)/(36a) are related to the structures (37a)/(37b) below respectively by a syntactic formation (or a semantic interpretation) of comparatives:

---

⁴One piece of evidence comes from the fact that the NP marked with <u>yori</u> can precede the other NP in all contexts, but the other order is not always possible.
   (i) Boku wa Tokyo yori Kobe ni sumi-tai.
       I   TOP   than   LOC live-want
     'I want to live in Kobe rather than in Tokyo.'
   (ii)*? Boku wa Kobe ni Tokyo (ni) yori sumi-tai.
It seems that NP-<u>yori</u> can be postposed only when the other NP's case is either nominative or accusative (cf. the following footnote).

(37)

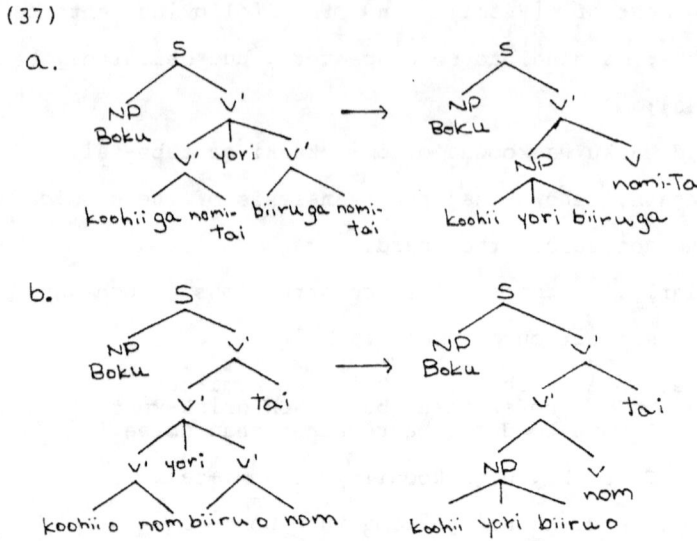

And finally, the rule responsible for the constituent order of (35b) and (36b) can be postulated as a movement of the comparative phrase NP-yori to the position next to V which is sister to the other NP under comparison:[5]

---

[5] There is no space to discuss the validity of the analysis as shown in (36), but let me mention a few points of relevance. First, the stipulation NP-yori NP-(ga) is a constituent while NP-(ga) NP-yori is not is supported by the fact that the former can be the asserted element in a cleft construction (which can contain only one NP), while the latter cannot.
 (i) Boku ga nomi-tai no wa koohii yori biiru da.
     I NOM drink-wantCOMPTOP cof. than beer COP
     'What I want to drink is beer rather than coffee.'
 (ii) *Boku ga nomi-tai no wa biiru ga/o koohii yori da.
Secondly, this comparative phrase attachment to V' bears some similarity to so-called 'quantifier floating' in the sense that a degree/quantity expression (adverbial) attaches

(38)

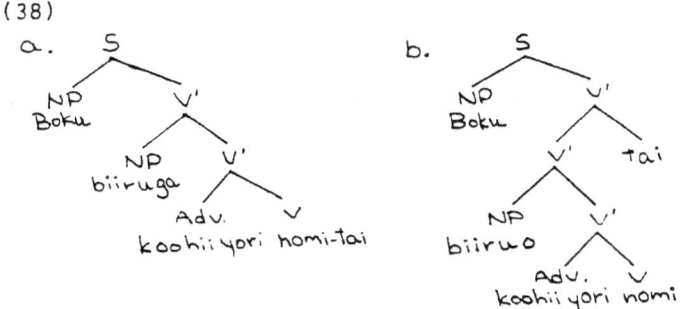

Now we can pinpoint what is wrong with (36b). As shown in (38b), the moved NP-yori modifies only the verb and not V-tai, unlike the case in (36a)/(38a), giving the wrong semantic scope.[6] To summarize this rather complex line of discussion, we can say that the crucial difference between (35b) and (36b) is that the scope of the comparative phrase

---

to the V', and in both cases the movement is largely restricted to the cases when the 'host' NP of the adverbial (before it moves) bears either nominative or accusative case. And finally, the stipulation that the moved NP-yori is a modifier to V is consistent with the use of yori as a comparative prefix to various predicates, which is most likely to be due to a reanalysis of this particle from a postposition to a prefix as illustrated below:
 [[x yori] ookii] ---> yori-ookii 'bigger'
where x is arbitrary or understood.

[6]Contrast (36b) with the following, where the adverb takusan 'much' makes the verb appropriate for comparative construction, and hence the sentence with the same word order becomes acceptable.
 (i) Boku wa biiru o koohii yori takusan nomi-tai.
 'I want to drink greater amount of beer than coffee.'

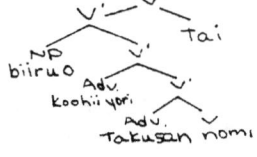

NP-yori is V + tai in (35a) while it is V alone in (36b). Again, this piece of data can follow from our hypothesis about the reanalysis of this suffixation but not from the previous analysis.

5.3. The distance between the verb and -tai

Shibatani (1979) notices that -tai attached to a 'complex verb' cannot readily allow the nominative marking on the second NP: (his examples)

(39) a. Kondo wa kono hon *?ga/o yomi-hazime-tai.
next TOP this book NOM ACC read-begin-want
'I want to start reading this book next.'

b. Kimi ni kono hon *?ga/o yonde yari-tai.
you DAT this book NOM ACC read give-want.
'I want to read this book for you.'

Shibatani suggests that this condition is basically the same as the one discussed in 4.2; the distance between the second NP and -tai. We saw in Section 4.2 that the distance condition is not so much a matter of distance as a matter of whether the intervening element is subcategorized by the verb alone or V- tai. The auxiliary verb hazime 'to begin' combines with V', kono hon o yom-, at the relevant level when the morphological operation of the suffixation occurs, hence it enforces the constituency of V', making it harder for the reanalysis of V'- tai to V- tai to take place. Similarly, with (39b), yaru combines with V', hon o yomu, yielding the same result.[7] The following shows the structure

---

[7]There is a morphological difference between hazimeru and yaru. The former combines with the infinitive form of the

at the relevant level.

(40)

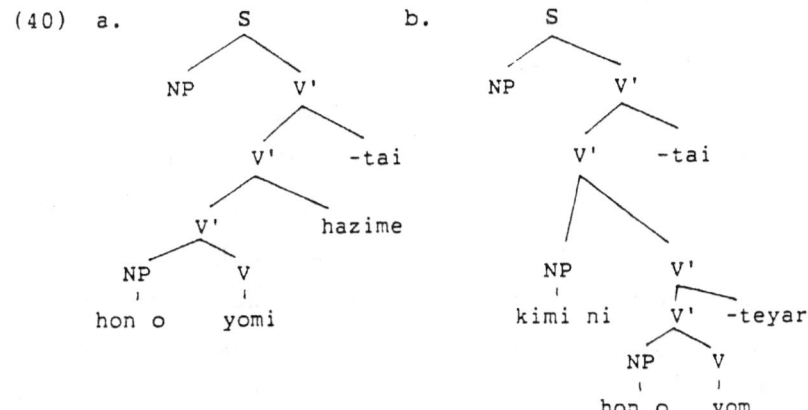

Other auxiliary verbs -oeru, -te simau 'finish' etc. behave the same way since they also combine with V'.

5.4. Semantic conditions

It has been noted, not so much in the generative approach but in the traditional work on Japanese that there is a semantic difference between NP-o V-tai and NP-ga V-tai. Hence there are some cases where all of the above-mentioned conditions are met and yet the nominative marking on the second NP is not natural. For instance, the difference between the following sentences is noted in Morita (1981):

---

verb, while the latter combines with the gerundive form (V-te). Strictly speaking, then, yomi-hazimeru is one word while yonde yaru are two words. Since they both combine with V' (their subject NP must be coreferent with that of the verb they combine with), this differnece is not relevant to the discussion here and is not reflected in (40).

(41) a. Mizu ga nomi-tai.
     b. Mizu o nomi-tai.
        water   drink-want   'I want to drink water.'

(42) a.*?Hae ga korosi-tai.
     b. Hae o korosi-tai.
        fly   kill-want   'I want to kill a fly.'

Morita explains this difference by saying that with NP- <u>ga</u> V-<u>tai</u> the focus is on the NP, while with NP-<u>o</u> V-<u>tai</u> it is the verb that is in focus. Thus (42a) is not natural in normal context because one does not have desire for killing something first and then picks a fly as the object. Along the same line, Yoshida (1971) suggests that (41a) is more stative and (41b) is more active.

Our approach to these constructions can capture this difference as part of the condition for the reanalysis to take place. When <u>tai</u> is interpreted as attaching to V', as in (41b) and (42b), the whole action denoted by V' is the content of desire. On the other hand, through the reanalysis of the predicate, the NP(which is now marked nominative) is brought into focus, since it is reanalyzed as the argument of V-tai, i.e., the object of desire. It is then no surprise that with most of the instances of the pattern NP-<u>ga</u> V-<u>tai</u>, the verb is semantically associated, or unmarked with the particular object it occurs with, such as <u>nomu</u> 'drink' for <u>mizu</u> 'water', <u>miru</u> 'watch' for <u>terebi</u> 'TV', etc.

As we mentioned at the beginning of this section, we cannot find these conditions as discussed above to equally apply to the alternation between NP-ga V-reru and NP-o V-reru. (See discussion in 6.1 for this point.) On the other hand, the two patterns do differ in the context they can appear in. Roughly speaking, the nominative pattern is used to express ability that is more permanent and inherent while the accusative pattern is used to express ability that is more temporary and circumstantial. See the following pair of examples:

(43) a. Taroo wa umaretuki koe ga/*o das-e-nai.
      TOP from birth voice   utter-able-not
  'Taro cannot make voice from birth.'

   b. Odoroki no amari, koe ga/o das-e-nak-atta.
      surprise too   voice utter-able-not-PAST
  'With too much surprise, I could not utter a sound.'

(44) a. Kare wa sake ga/*?o nom-e-nai.
      he TOP sake   drink-able-not
  'He cannot drink sake.'

   b. Kyoo wa sukinadake sake ga/o nom-eru.
      todayTOP at will   sake   drink-able
  'Today we can drink as much sake as we want.'

According to our assumption the difference comes from the different scope of -reru, namely, [NP-o V]-reru and [NP-ga] [V-reru]. In the former, the whole V'-reru is a stative predicate that predicates on the subject NP in the latter, since V-reru is now reanalysed as a predicate which applies to the second NP of the sentence, the predicate V-reru is interpreted as a property of the second NP ('NP is V-able') which, as a complex predicate, is predicated on the first NP. It follows then that the latter form with the nominative-marked second NP is used to express ability as a property (as in (43a), (44a)), while the former form with the accusative-marked second NP cannot be.

6. Concluding remarks and some issues
6.1. Basic and derived case patterns for stative predicates

Let us summarize our findings in this section. Two-place predicates in Japanese form two classes; [+stative] predicates are basically subcategorized for the case frame [NP-ni NP-ga V], while [-stative] predicates are subcategorized for the case frame [NP-ga NP-o V]. These basic case patterns are also proposed by Kuroda (1979) and are called 'ergative' and 'accusative' respectively. Of all the stative predicates (for instance, among those listed in Kuno (1973: 90-91)), we find that the ones which can never occur with the dative-marked first NP (i.e., in the ergative pattern) are either the cases of reanalyzed stative predicates discussed above, or the predicates expressing 'being good/bad at x', which can be shown not to be two place predicate (see Chapter III, Section 2.2. for the arguments).[8] This leads us to conclude that double nominative case marking that occurs with two-place stative predicates is not a basic case pattern in the sense that no simple two place predicate subcategorize for two nominative NP's. The case pattern [NP-ga NP-ga V] with stative

---

[8] Although Kuno (1973) says that a number of the predicates from this list cannot occur with NP-ni, in fact all of them can in certain contexts except for the ones mentioned above.

predicates is derived either by the reanalysis process on the suffixed predicate as discussed above or by the independently motivated rule of ni-->ga conversion.

Our claims can be illustrated as the following:

Accusative	double Nom.	Ergative
NPga [NPo V]-tai -->	NPga NPga V-tai	-
NPga [NPo suk]-i da-->	NPga NPga suki-da	-
NPga [NPo hosi]-i -->	NPga NPga hosi-i	-
NPga [NPo V]-reru -->	NPga NPga V-reru<--	NPni NPga V-reru
NPga NPo wakaru(1)	NPga NPga wakaru(2)<-	NPni NPga wakaru(2)
	NPga NPga dekiru <--	NPni NPga dekiru
	NPga NPga kowai <--	NPni NPga kowai

This chart explains a number of facts: (1) the accusative pattern with stative predicates is possible only with derived predicates by suffixation; (2) all basic stative predicates can take both ergative and double nominative case pattern (3) except for -reru (see below) suffixed predicates cannot take the ergative case pattern; (4) nothing is exceptional about wakaru once we postulate two different verbs with different value for the feature [stative]; (5) [NP-ni NP-o V] never occurs either basic or derived.

Some supplementary remarks are in order. First, we notice that V-reru is the only predicate that allows all three case patterns. It is not plausible to classify V-reru into two types as we did for wakaru, because even when it occurs with the accusative pattern it cannot take imperative ending which is the sign of the feature [-stative]. It seems then that the suffix -reru can basically attach to both V' and V. This situation can be perceived in the following way. V'-reru (45a) goes through the reanalysis (45b), and its V-reru part gets lexicalized as belonging to the same class as other simple stative predicates (45c):[9]

(45) a. Taroo ga [kono hon o yom]-eru.
            this book read
'Taro can read this book.'

b. Taroo ga kono hon ga [yom-eru].

c. Taroo ni kono hon ga [yomeru].

In this connection it is interesting to note that there exist a few lexicalized V-reru forms for instance, mi-eru, kiko-eru. (Historically they are derived from the old potential form of miru, kiku -- miyu, kikoyu). These forms

---

[9]Okutsu (1983) cites a statistical study by Tsuchiya (1971, monthly report publised by NHK, which I could not get hold of), which tested the speakers' feelings about the appropriateness of the alternating case markings with tai, reru. The percentage of the speakers who found the particular case marking more appropriate than the other is reported to be as the following for each pattern:
Mizu o nomi-tai: 52% / mizu ga nomi-tai: 46.6%
Eigo o hanas-eru:26.6% / Eigo ga hanas-eru:72.3%
It is consistent with our analysis that the judgements are almost equally divided for tai, while the nominative case is more popular with reru. We can conjecture that this is because, as discussed above, V-reru belongs to the ergative paradigm, which makes the nominative marking on the second NP more unmarked than it is with tai.
One question that remains here is the following: why is it that V -reru can have the ergative case pattern (presumably via lexicalization) while V - tai cannot. One can speculate that one reason comes from the fact that the potential suffix is closely related to the inchoative ending in the transitivity paradigm (e.g., yak-u / yak-eru 'bake'), as discussed in Jacobsen (1980). Further discussion must be left for future research.

occur only with the ergative pattern and double nominative pattern, and contrast with the transparent forms, <u>mir-eru</u> and <u>kik-eru</u>, which occur with all three patterns.

Secondly, we have noted that for <u>suki-da</u>, <u>kirai-da</u>, and <u>hosii</u>, the double nominative pattern is more natural than the presumably basic accusative pattern. It is quite natural that due to the unproductiveness of the suffixation the 'reanalyzed' forms are present in the lexicon as such, making the accusative pattern more marked. This approach also accounts for the varied judgements among speakers for the preferrence on the case patterns. We may say that for those who allow the accusative pattern more readily, the suffixation is more transparent. It is notable in this respect that Shibatani (1978) cites some examples of <u>hosii</u> occuring with accusative-marked NP taken from Matsumura's (1957) study of Tokugawa period (17th-19th C.) Japanese. This shows that the accusative pattern is not a new phenomena based on the analogy or back formation.

The third and last point about the chart above is the assumption that the double nominative pattern is a derived case marking pattern in the grammar of Japanese. In the generative grammatical studies on case markings in Japanese there is a well-known controversy about whether we should have the double nominative pattern as basic or the ergative pattern as basic. In either case one has to be derived from the other in some instances. There is no space for going into the controversy here, and, as Kuno (1978) notes, the resolution may not be reached for years to come. For the range of data that we are concerned with here, however, we are led to believe that the ergative pattern is the basic one. There are a couple of advantages for doing so. First, it is compatible with the fact that while all the ergative pattern sentences with stative predicates can alternate with double nominative sentences, the reverse is not true, i.e., that is not possible for those reanalyzed predicates. Secondly, it implies that while the ergative case pattern is a basic one the double nominative pattern is a derived one. This seems desirable from the point of view of universal grammar. A predicate subcategorizing for two nominative case NP's is a problem for any kind of case theory. Japanese also has a general blocking on double case marking for accusative and dative cases, which is functionally motivated. Thus it seems more desirable if we could view the double nominative pattern as not basic.[10]

---

[10]Kuroda (1980) postulates the basic case oattern for Japanese to be intransitive [NP-ga V], accusative [NP-ga NP-o V], and ergative [NP-ni NP-ga V], but mentions that the double nominative pattern of hosii, suki-da, kirai-da, V-tai must be treated as exceptions. The analysis presented here offers some explanation for their exceptional nature.

6.2. On the object-hood of the second NP

We have been avoiding the use of the term 'object' to refer to the second NP of the stative predicate constructions above. Although the term has been used (as in 'nominative-marked object NP'), it is not clear whether they are indeed object or not. However, as long as we maintain the ergative pattern to be basic for simple stative predicates, abolishing o-->ga conversion, there is no reason to assume the second NP of those predicates to be the object NP. Tonoike (1976-77) also points out that all the stative predicates are intransitive and call the pattern 'dative intransitive'. On the other hand, for those stative predicates that are considered to be a result of the reanalysis here, namely, for those for which there exist alternating case markings on the second NP, this is not so clear.

Kuroda (1983) recently pointed out that now we have evidence for believing that the second NP of V- tai and hosii is subject, citing Saito (1983). Saito (1983) argues for the subjecthood of the second NP with the stative predicate showing that these NP's can undergo the putative rule of 'subject-to-object raising'. For instance,

(46) a. Minna ni(wa) Y-sensei ga kowai.
　　　 all　　　　 prof.Y.　　 fearful
　　'Everybody is afraid of Prof. Y.'

b. Minna ga Y-sensei o kowai to omotteiru.
　　 all　　 prof. Y. fearful COMP think
　　'Everybody believes Prof. Y to be terrifying.'

The second NP 'Prof. Y' can be argued to be the subject of (46a) because it can be 'raised' to the object position of the higher sentence as in (46b).

Kuroda (1983) says that the same raising can apply to the nominative marked second NP of predicates such as <u>hosii</u> and V-<u>tai</u>.

(47) a. Taroo wa sono hon ga yomi-tai.
              that book   read-want
    'Taro wants to read that book.'

    b. Taroo wa sono hon o yomi-tai to ommoteiru.
       TarooTOP that book ACC read-wantCOMP think
       'Taro feels the desire to read that book.'

(48) a. Taroo wa sono hon ga hosii.
       TaroTOP that book NOM want
       'Taro wants that book.'

    b. Taroo wa sono hon o hosii to omotteiru.
       'Taro feels the desire for that book.'

Although Kuroda (1983) says that this is evidence for the subjecthood of the second NP in (47a) and (48a), there are reasons to believe that this test does not prove that. The problem is that there is another source for (47b) and (48b) which does not involve raising, namely, the accusative marking on the second NP in (47a) and (48a) is possible. Further, there is evidence that the accusative NP's in (47b) and (48b) are not the object NP of the whole sentence. The object NP of the ordinary raising construction(such as 46b) is passivizable, but the NP's in (47b) and (48b) are not. See the following:

(49) a. Y-sensei wa minna ni kowai to omow-are-teiru.
       Prof. Y   all   terrifying COMPthink-PASS-STAT
       'Prof. Y is considered by all to be terrifying.'

b. *? Sono hon wa minna ni yomitai to omow-are-teiru.
   that book   all   read-want COMP think-PASS
   'That book is wanted (for reading) by everybody.'

c. ?? Sono hon wa minna ni hosii to omow-are-teiru.
   'That book is considered to be desirable by all.'

(cf. d. Sono hon wa minna ni omoshiroi to omow-are-teiru.)
     that book   all   interesting COMP-think-PASS
     'That book is considered to be interesting by all.'

Contrast the perfectly acceptable passive version of the raised construction (49a) and (49d) with (49b) and (49c). We are led to conclude that the nominative marked second NP of a derived stative predicate is not the subject.

Now, using the same line of argument, we can show that with the other stative predicates which we claim to be the result of reanalysis the second NP cannot be proven to be the subject of the predicate, because they cannot go under raising:

(50) a. Taroo wa Hanako ga sukida.
        'Taro likes Hanako.'

   b. Taroo wa Hanako o sukida to omotteiru.
      'Taro feels he likes Hanako.'

   c. *?Hanako wa Taroo ni sukida to omow-are-teiru.
      'Hanako is considered by Taro to be his favorite.'

(cf. d. Hanako wa Taroo ni baka-da to omow-are-teiru.
                          fool   COMP think-PASS
     'Hanako is considered to be a fool by Taro.')

(51) a. Minna ni kono hon ga yomeru.
        all   this book read-able
        'Everybody can read this book.'

   b. Minna ga kono hon o yomeru to omotteiru.
      'Everybody consideres this book to be readable.'

   c. ??Kono hon wa minna ni yomeru to omow-are-teiru.
      'This book is considered (by all) to be readable.'

(cf.d. Kono hon wa minna ni yasasii to omow-are-teiru.
'This book is considered to be easy by everybody.)
(See the relevant discussion with a transitivizing suffix Adj- garu in Chapter III.)

The discussion above has made it clear that the nominative-marked second NP of the derived stative predicates cannot be considered to be the subject NP as in the case of the nominative NP of the simple stative predicate. This observation is in accordance with our contention that this nominative marking is not basic but is a result of reanalysis.

6.3. The accusative NP condition--a problem

We have claimed that the double nominative case pattern with derived stative predicates is a result of reanalysis of the following: [NP-o V]-suff.--->[NP-ga] [V-suff.]. We have claimed that these suffixes basically attach to V', and when certain conditions are met the reanalysis applies. It is predicted then that the latter construction is more marked. Although it is not so clear with -reru as discussed above, it indeed is the case with -tai, according to what is reported in Yoshida (1971). He gives a count of all occurrences of -tai in a novel I am a Cat by Sooseki Natsume. Of the 155 occurrences of this suffix, NP- ga V-tai was 16, NP-o V-tai was 41, NP-ni V-tai 9, NP-e V-tai 7, and others 82. Also, a remark from Kobayashi (1922) is cited in Shibatani (1978) that the nominative marking with

-tai and -reru seems to be a rather modern usage. Our analysis predicts these findings.

There remains one important question, however. Why is it that only accusative NP can be assigned nominative case as a result of this reanalysis? In other words, why is it that we do not have the following pairs of sentences as alternatives?

(52) a. Boku wa yotto ni/*ga nor-eru.
     I TOP yacht LOC   ride-able
    'I can ride on a yacht.'

b. Boku wa kooen de/*ga asobi-tai.
   I TOP part LOC   play-want
  'I want to play in the park.'

Let us look at another type of construction with a similar property. It does not involve a stative predicate but rather an aspectual auxiliary -te-aru. The following example shows the alternation in case marking.

(53) a. Boku wa yado o yoyaku-si-te-aru.
    I TOP room   reserve-PERF
   'I have reserved a room.'

b. Boku wa yado ga yoyaku-si-te-aru.

It is conceivable to expand our approach to these constructions as well:

(53) a. Boku wa [yado o yoyaku-si]-te-aru.

b. Boku wa [yado ga][yoyaku-si-te-aru].

In this analysis the alternating case marking is explained by the different elements this auxiliary can attach to; although te-aru is an auxiliary attaching basically to V''s, it can be reanalyzed as an intransitivizing suffix to the verb, changing the case marking of the preceding NP to nominative. One piece of evidence for postulating the structure as in (53) is found with the scope of time adverbs. Since -te-aru marks a perfective aspect, it cannot felicitously occur with a time adverb denoting definite past. However, a time adverb denoting past can occur if there is a V' unit where it can just modify the verb:

(54) a. Boku wa yado o kinoo yoyaku-si-te-aru.
       I TOP room yesterday reserve-PERF
     'I have reserved the room (yesterday).'

   b. *?Boku wa yado ga kinoo yoyaku-si-te-aru.

If the time adverb is perfective, then it can occur with the reanalyzed V- te-aru:

(55) a. Boku wa yado ga sude ni yoyaku-si-te-aru.
       I room already reserve-PERF
     'I have already reserved the room.'

So the condition here is parallel to the distance condition we discussed above; if V+suff. is reanalyzed as a predicate, the preceding NP and the predicate cannot be separated by the element which is in the scope of the verb alone.

Now let us go back to the main topic of this subsection; namely, -te-aru constructions also require the NP to be accusative-marked in order for the reanalysis, or the alternating case pattern, to exist, as shown below:

(56) a. Kyoo wa kaimono ni/*ga it-te-aru.
      todayTOP shopping GOAL go-PERF
     'I have done (lit. been to) shopping today.'

   b. Kyoo wa kaimono o/ga sumase-te-aru.
      todayTOP shopping finish-PERF
     'I have done shopping today.'

We have seen that the reanalyzed stative predicate and -te-aru construction have what we may call 'the accusative condition'. This situation is different from that of the 'tough' predicate constructions, where any oblique case in the 'lower' clause can be marked with nominative case (cf. Inoue (1978), Saito (1982), Kuroda (1983)). See the following example from Kuroda (1983), to which Kuroda assigns the structure (57b):

(57) a. LA kara ga karera ga Tokyo e iki-yasyi.
LA from   they   GOAL go easy
'LA is easy for them to go to Tokyo from.'

b. [LA kara ga [karera ga Tokyo e t iki]-yasui]

Kuroda says that the fact the postposition kara 'from' can occur with nominative case is 'good evidence that LA is moved out of the embedded sentence.' Kuroda further claims that the NP that occurs in that position is the subject of the higher predicate -yasui. He bases his argument on the raising construction, but he uses a sentence where an accusative or nominative NP is moved to the higher sentence. In fact, if we embed (57) in a construction where the raising can apply (cf. 58a), we find that the raising cannot yield an acceptable sentence(58b), which suggests that LA is not a full-fledged subject of -yasui.

(58) a. Karera wa [LA kara ga Tokyo e iki-yasui] to omou.

b.*Karera wa LA kara o Tokyo e iki-yasui to omou.
   they   from   to go easy COMP think
'They consider LA to be easy to go to Tokyo from.'

It seems that a structure where LA is outside the sentence is more plausible (cf. Saito (1982)).

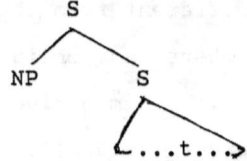

Note that this is also the structure for topicalization structure.

On the other hand, we do not want to give the same analysis to the nominative marking on the second NP of derived stative predicates and te-aru construction, because there is no reason to assume that the nominative NP comes from the 'lower' clause; unlike the case with the 'tough' predicate constructions, no oblique NP nor even dative NP can be marked with a nominative case in the reanalyzed structure.[11]

---

[11] Saito (1982) proposes to treat the nominative-marked second NP of the potential -reru constructions as focus NP in a way parallel to that of 'tough' sentences. He gives some examples such as the following, where the parallelism holds:
  (i) Kotosi wa yooroppa ga yasuku ik-eru.
      this year Europe   cheap   go-able
      'It is Europe that we can go cheaply this year.'
Saito claims that all occurrences of nominative-marked second NP's with stative predicates can be treated as focus NP. However, the parallelism is only partial; unless the potential predicate is modified with some adverb such as yasuku 'cheap', kantan ni 'easily', etc. oblique NP cannot be marked with a nominative case:
  (ii) Yooroppa *ga/ni ik-eru nante urayamasii.
       Europe   go-able COMP envious
       '(I'm) envious (of you) that you can go to Europe.'
Also, -tai and -te-aru do not allow non-accusative NP to be nominative-marked in the reanalyzed construction under any

As for the reason why V' containing only an accusative NP allows the reanalysis, we can only speculate that whatever the reason is, it probably has to do with the fact that nominative and accusative seem to be the grammatically assigned case (as opposed to semantically assigned case) in Japanese (cf. Kuroda (1979)). The clarification of this point awaits further research.

---

circumstance. Thus it seems necessary that we keep separate the focus NP that appears in the 'tough' constructions and the nominative-marked second NP's that we have been discussing in this section.

CHAPTER V

PHRASAL SUFFIXES II

In the previous chapters we have seen a number of constructions in Japanese which can be best analyzed as a morphological operation applying to a syntactically derived phrase. In particular, one consequence of phrasal suffixation in the form of reanalysis was discussed in the previous chapter and was demonstrated to account for some facts of case alternations, which could not be otherwise given a plausible account. In this chapter we will examine a few more suffixes that can be analyzed as attaching to a unit larger than a verb, and discuss the merits of such an approach. In Section 1 two verbal suffixes which syntactically attach to a V' phrase will be examined in terms of their scopes and in comparison with their corresponding English expressions. In Section 2 we will discuss some nominalizing suffixes which attach to a phrase and form predicate nominals, and in Section 3 we will examine some subordination suffixes. In Section 4, a new approach to the morphology of passive constructions will be suggested, based on the assumption pursued in this work that the domain of suffixation can be flexible across lexical and phrasal levels.

1. Suffixes with phrasal scopes

1.1. Reciprocal suffix -au

Japanese has a verbal suffix -au which expresses the reciprocal action between plural (usually two) agents. The following example illustrates its property in a simple form:

(1) a. Taroo ga Hanako o hagemasi-ta.
      NOM   ACC cheer up-PAST
   'Taro cheered up Hanako.'

   b. Taroo to Hanako ga hagemasi-at-ta.
         and   NOM cheer up-REC-PAST
   'Taro and Hanako cheered up each other.'

We can say that this suffix attaches to a transitive verb and creates an intransitive verb that requires a plural subject in the same way as do such simple verbs as tatakau 'to fight', kekkon-suru 'to marry', and so on. This can be schematically stated as the following:

(2) V-au (x & y) --> V (x, y) & V (y, x)

What is of interest to our concern here is the fact that what can fill the transitive verb slot V in (2) is not restricted to the simple verbs but can be a verb and its arguments. Consider the following examples.

(3) a. Taroo ga Hanako ni ryoosin o syookai-si-ta.
         NOM   ACC parents ACC introduce-PAST
   'Taro introduced his parents to Hanako.'

   b. Taroo to Hanako ga ryoosin o syookai-si-at-ta.
         and   NOM parents ACC introduce-REC-PAST
   'Taro and Hanako introduced their respective parents to each other.'

(4) a. Taroo ga Hanako ni isi o butuke-ta.
         NOM   DAT stoneACC throw at-PAST
   'Taro threw a stone at Hanako.'

b. Taroo to Hanako ga isi o butuke-at-ta.
         and   NOM stone ACC throw-REC-PAST
   'Taro and Hanako threw a stone at each other.'

(5) a. Taroo ga Hanako no waruguti o it-ta.
          NOM   GEN bad words ACC speak-PAST
       'Taro spoke ill of Hanako.'

   b. Taroo to Hanako ga waruguti o ii-at-ta.
           and   NOM bad words ACC speak-REC-PAST
      'Taro and Hanako spoke ill of each other.'

As can be gathered from the English translation, the V slots in these sentences are filled by V''s: <u>ryoosin o syookai-suru</u>, <u>isi o butukeru</u>, and <u>waruguti o iu</u>. Even though they are not a simple verb, they notionally constitute a complex predicate that expresses an action that is directed to a patient. What can constitute a 'complex predicate' in this sense seems to be a semantic (and pragmatic) matter rather than syntactic, as shown by the contrast below:

(6) a. Gohho to Googyan ga (otagai no) syoozoo o kaki-at-ta.
       G. and G. NOM each other's portrait ACC paint-REC
       'van Gogh and Gauguin painted portraits of e. o.'

   b. *? G. to G. ga (otagai no) syoozoo o moyasi-at-ta.
      '*? van Gogh and Gauguin burned portraits of e. o.'

This type of contrast is also observed in the parallel English constructions with the reciprocal pronoun, as shown in the translations above, as well as in the Wh-movement construction:

(7) a. Who did van Gogh paint a portrait of?

   b. *? Who did van Gogh burn a portrait of?

The pronoun <u>otagai</u> that appears in (6) has a distribution that overlaps with <u>-au</u> but is supplementary to <u>each other</u> in part. When the predicate denotes a direct physical action, this pronoun is awkward.

(8) Taroo to Hanako ga (*?otagai o) naguri-at-ta.
    and   NOM   each other hit   REC-PAST
'Taro and Hanako hit each other.'

(9) Taroo to Hanako ga (*otagai o) daki-at-ta.
    and   NOM   each other hug-REC-PAST
'Taro and Hanako hugged each other.'

On the other hand, when it denotes a non-physical (mental or verbal) act, the presence of this pronoun is more natural.

(10) Taroo to Hanako ga (otagai o) nagusame-at-ta.
    and   NOM   each other console-REC-PAST
'Taro and Hanako consoled each other.'

Further, the pronoun in (9) cannot take over the function of the reciprocal suffix while it can in (10):

(11) a. *Taroo to Hanako ga otagai o dai-ta.
       'Taro and Hanako hugged each other.'

    b. Taroo to Hanako ga otagai o nagusame-ta.
       'Taro and Hanako consoled each other.'

The following examples show that the complex predicate to which this reciprocal suffix attaches can involve an embedded clause:

(12) a. T to H ga [*(otagai ga) matigat-teiru] to ii(at)ta.
     and   NOM   e.o. NOM be mistaken   COMP say-REC
     'T. and H. said (to each other) that the other
     person is mistaken.'

    b. T to H ga [*(otagai ga) buzi-ka] o tazune(at)ta.
     and NOM e.o. NOM safe whether ACC ask-REC-PAST
     'T and H asked (each other) whether the other
     person was safe and well.'

Consider, however, the following:

(13) *T to H ga [otagai ga matigat-teiru] to omoi-at-ta.
                                            sinzi-at-ta.
                                            kanzi-at-ta.
       and NOM   e.o. NOM be mistaken COMP believed/felt
       'T and H believed that each other was mistaken.'
              (cf. OK with omot-ta/ sinzi-ta/ kanzi-ta)

The difference between the main verbs of (12) and those of (13) is that the former subcategorizes for an indirect object as well as a clausal object, while the latter takes only a clausal object. Consider their corresponding non-reciprocal sentences.

(14) a. T ga H ni [kanozyo ga matigat-teiru] to it-ta.
        nom DAT she   NOM be mistaken COMP said
        'T said to H that she was mistaken.'

     b. T ga [H ga matigat-teiru] to omotta.
        NOM NOM be mistaken COMP believed
        'T believed that H was mistaken.'

It then turns out that the 'complex predicate' to which -au attaches is a syntactic constituent (clausal object + V) in (12), while it is not so in (13) (clause minus SU + V). This point is further confirmed by the contrast between (13) and its 'raised' version, where the complex predicate can be analyzed as a constituent.

(15) T to H ga (otagai o) tensai da to omoi-at-teiru.
     and NOM   e.o. ACC genious COP COMP believe-REC
     'T and H believe each other to be a genious.'

Note that when there is an embedded clause involved, the presence of the pronoun otagai becomes mandatory, and when -au can be attached, the pronoun by itself takes on the function of expressing reciprocity (cf. 12). We can consider this difference to follow from the different principles according to which purely phrasal operations (i.e., syntactic) and morphological operations apply. Namely, the suffix -au, being an element of a morphological operation, requires its host to be a constituent (in this case V'), while the interpretation of pronoun otagai can involve non-constituents, being a syntactic rule.

We can now characterize the constructions with this reciprocal suffix as the following. The suffix -au attaches to a predicate P1 (complex or simple) that can be analyzed as an action directed to a patient NP, and creates a predicate that takes a plural subject NP corresponding to the agent and the patient NP's of P1. Besides its semantic restrictions P1 must meet the structural condition of being a constituent. In regard to this last point, let us consider (5) above, repeated here:

(16) a. Taroo ga Hanako no waruguti o it-ta.
NOM   GEN bad words ACC said
'Taro spoke ill of Hanako.'

b. Taroo to Hanako ga waruguti o ii-at-ta.
and   NOM bad words ACC say-REC-PAST
'Taro and Hanako spoke ill of each other.'

The patient NP (in genitive case) of (16a) that appears as part of the conjoined subject NP in (16b) constitute N' rather than V', since a genitive NP cannot be an argument of a verb but occurs as a modifier to the head noun, as shown below. Also note the ungrammaticality of moving this NP away from its head noun as shown in (17b).

(17) a. Taroo wa [Hanako no [waruguti]]N' o it-ta.

b. *Hanako no Taroo wa waruguti o it-ta.

It turns out then that the putative complex predicate to which -au attaches in (16b) is not a constituent. One way of handling this that immediately comes to mind is to treat this non-constituent as a reanalyzed predicate on a par with such English expressions as take advantage of. There exists more evidence to support the stipulation that the non-constituent in (17) must be recognized as a constituent at some level. Note how passivization and right node raising apply to a sentence like (17):

(18) a. Hanako wa Taroo ni waruguti o iw-are-ta.
       TOP   DAT bad words ACC say-PASS-PAST
   'Hanako was spoken ill of by Taro.'

b. T wa H no, Jiroo wa Hiroko no waruguti o it-ta.
   TOP GEN   TOP   GEN bad words ACC said
   'Taro spoke ill of Hanako, and Jiro, Hiroko.'

Regular passivization (as opposed to adversative passivization) has been customarily assumed to apply only to the direct and indirect object NP, and hence the passive construction like (18a) where the subject NP occupies the genitive NP position in the corresponding active sentence has been treated as an adversative passive construction. We will not go into the discussion of the long-standing issues surrounding Japanese passives (see Section 4), but only note here that given such evidence as (16a) and (18b), it is not implausible to consider the restructuring of a construction like (17) as the following:

(19) Taroo wa Hanako no [waruguti o it]-ta.

One salient condition on this restructuring (and most likely its motivization) is that the genitive NP must be interpreted as the patient in relation to the complex predicate to be reanalyzed. This condition seems quite conceivably a pragmatic one, dependent on the context. Thus compare the following structurally parallel sentences:

(20) a. Taroo wa Hanako no haha o nikun-da.
         TOP   GEN mother ACC hated
    'Taro hated Hanako's mother.'

   b. Taroo wa Hanako no kodomo o home-ta.
         TOP   GEN child ACC praised
    'Taro praised Hanako's child.'

The putative complex predicate in (20a), namely, 'hate the mother of (x)' can hardly be an action directed to x, while that of (20b) 'praise the child of (x)' can. This subtle difference is reflected in the fact that (20a) cannot passivize nor have a corresponding reciprocal construction while (20b) can:

(21) a. *? Hanako wa Taroo ni haha o nikum-are-ta.
              TOP   DAT mother ACC hate-PASS-PAST
    'Taro hated Hanako's mother (on Hanako).'

   b. *?T to H wa (otagai no) haha o nikumi-at-ta.
          and TOP   e.o. GEN mother ACC hate-REC-PAST
    'Taro and Hanako hated each other's mother.'

(22) a. Hanako wa Taroo ni kodomo o home-rare-ta.
            TOP   DAT child ACC praise-PASS-PAST
    'Taro praised Hanako's child (to her).'

   b. T to H wa (otagai no) kodomo o home-at-ta.
         and TOP   e.o. GEN child ACC praise-REC-PAST
    'Taro and Hanako praised each other's child.'

Aside from the rather subtle cases such as (20b) above, there exist in Japanese a large number of expressions that require this restructuring, one particularly productive pattern consisting of a patient NP in the genitive case, his/her body parts in the accusative case, and a verb. A few examples are given below:

(23) a. x no sewa o suru 'to take care of x'

b. x no kigen o toru 'to flatter x's feelings'

c. x no kata o tataku 'to pat x's shoulder'

d. x no atama o naderu 'to pat x's head'

In sum we can say that the reciprocal suffix -au attaches to a semantically (and pragmatically) defined transitive V' constituent. We will lastly note one interesting point about the nominalization of the derived reciprocal predicates. As we have discussed earlier, Japanese has a rather productive Ø-nominalization on the infinitival form of a verb, with which the subject or the object NP's appear in the genitive case. This nominalization can apply to reciprocal predicates as well:

(24) a. Taroo to Hanako no naguri-ai
        amd   GEN hit-REC
'T and H's hitting each other'

b. Taroo to Hanako no waruguti no ii-ai
      and   GEN bad words GEN say-REC
'T and H's speaking ill of each other'

While the nominalization of (24a) is straightforward, in (24b) the scope of this suffix is not properly represented under the nominalization. Namely, the constituent waruguti o iu is broken up and only the verb+suffix is nominalized. Note that this form is in accordance with the NP structure of Japanese. What seems to be happening here is that a phrasal constituent which is preserved under suffixation ([waruguti o ii]-au) is nominalized as an ordinary verb phrase ([waruguti o] [ii-au]). We will see the same phenomena with another suffix -sugiru that will be taken up in the next section, which presents an interesting contrast in its nominalized forms depending on the position of the nominal.

1.2. On the suffix -sugiru

The morpheme sugiru is a word as well as a suffix. As an independent word it means 'to pass (by)', as in toki ga sugiru 'time passes', or in kisya ga Osaka o sugi-ta 'the train passed by Osaka'. When it is attached to a verb as a suffix, it means 'excessively'. It is this suffix use that we will examine in this section in terms of its scope and other properties. We will also consider the English prefix with a similar meaning over- in this connection.

Let us first survey the various scopes this suffix can cover. Considering that the semantic contribution of -sugiru is to predicate the meaning of an excessively large quantity over a certain element in the sentence, we can classify its use by the semantic element it modifies in particular.

A. Frequency of action

(25) Taroo wa [gaisyoku o si]-sugiru.
   TOP eat-out ACC do excessively
   'Taro eats out too often.'

(26) Konogoro [ame ga huri]-sugiru.
    recently rainNOM fall excessively
    'Recently it rains too often.'

B. Degree of state

(27) Kono mati wa [sizuka]-sugiru. (AN)
    this town TOP quiet- exces.
    'It is too quiet in this town.'

(28) Taroo wa [waka]-sugiru. (A)
    TOP young exces.
    'Taro is too young.'

(29) Hanako wa [bizin]-sugiru. (N)
    TOP beauty exces.
    'Hanako is too much of a beauty.'

C. Adverb

(30) Yuube wa [osoku made oki-te i]-sugi-ta.
    last night late until stay up-PRG exces-PAST
    '(I) stayed up too late last night.'

(31) Taroo wa [takaku tobi]-sugi-ta.
    TOP high jump exces PAST
    'Taro jumped too high.'

D. Quantity

(32) Taroo wa [aisukuriimu o tabe]-sugi-ta.
    TOP icecream ACC eat exces PAST
    'Taro ate too much icecream.'

(33) Taroo wa [kane ga ari]-sugiru.
    TOP money NOM be exces
    'Taro has too much money.'

(34) Kono mati niwa [kooen ga sukuna]-sugiru.
    this town LOC-TOP park NOM few exces
    'There are too few parks in this town.'

These examples illustrate the versatility of this suffix.[1]

---

[1]Note that verbal compounds can be in the scope of -sugiru, in the parallel way to V'. Namely, the incorporated adverb of the compound can be modified by -sugiru.
   (i) Taroo wa taka-nozomi si-sugiru.
       high hope do exces.
   'Taro's hopes are too high.'

It can attach to verbs, adjectives, adjectival nouns, and even to a few cases of nouns (as in 29). Furthermore, it can attach to complex verbs of various sorts as shown below:

(35) Passive-causative
Taroo wa kaisya de [osoku made hatarak-ase-rare]-sugiru.
    TOP companyLOC late until work-CAUSE-PASS exces
'Taro is caused to work until too late at his work.'

(36) Negation
Taroo wa [nani mo sir-ana]-sugiru.
         nothing know-NEG exces
'Taro is too ignorant about anything'

(37) Honorification
Sensei wa [hon o o-yomi ni nari]-sugiru.
prof. TOP book ACC read-HONOR   exces
'The professor reads too many books.'

There is an adverb which has the same semantic function as this suffix: <u>amari-nimo</u> 'excessively'. Unlike the case of <u>-au</u> and <u>otagai</u> that we saw in Section 1.1., these two expressions seem to have exactly the same distribution. They can be both present in a sentence, or either one can replace the other; except that the suffix <u>sugiru</u> seems to be preferred in the actual usages, and <u>amari-nimo</u> is accompanied by a frequency adverb <u>yoku</u> or a quantity adverb <u>takusan</u> to specify its scope, as exemplified below.

(38) a. Hito ga amarinimo takusan iru.
        person NOM excessively many be
        'There are too many people.

   b. Hito ga takusan i-sugiru.

(ii) Kesa wa haya-oki si-sugi-ta.
     today TOP early-rising do excess.-PAST
     '(I) got up too early this morning.'

(39) a. Taroo wa amarinimo kasikoi.
         TOP excessively clever
    'Taro is too clever.'

   b. Taroo wa kasiko-sugiru.

(40) a. Kono kuruma wa amarinimo yoku kosyoo suru.
       this car TOP excessively often break-down do
    'This car breaks down too often.'

   b. Kono kuruma wa kosyoo si-sugiru.
       this car TOP break down do-exec
    'This car breaks down too often.'

It is under the V' node that frequency adverbs and quantity/degree adverbs occur, and it is natural to assume that a suffix of the same function attaches to the same level. It is, however, not clear for the examples such as (26), (34), and (38), where the subject NP is also in the scope of the suffix. One conceivable way of dealing with these data is to assume that -sugiru has a flexible domain and can attach to either V' or S. We will later see that there are more suffixes with this very property, and some interesting consequences can be drawn from that assumption. With those suffixes it will be shown that the semantic function of the suffix differs depending on whether it attaches to V' or S. With -sugiru, however, there seems to be no difference in its function whether it has the subject NP in its scope or not. Further, note that the sentences (26), (34), and (38), where the suffix has the subject NP in its scope are of the special types: namely, they are existential sentences and weather sentences, which in English do not have an underlying contentful subject NP. It may not be implausible to consider that these sentences are closer to V' than to S, and that it is the V' in this extended sense that <u>sugiru</u> can attach to. The question of how S and V' should be defined, however, is an issue much too complex to be pursued here, and we will only note this as a possible analysis for the suffixation of <u>-sugiru</u>.

We will now turn to the English prefix <u>over-</u> which is partially similar to the Japanese suffix <u>-sugiru</u>. <u>Over-</u> also attaches to verbs and adjectives, and add the meaning 'excessively' to the sentence. Roughly speaking, the meaning it contributes can be classified as the following.

(41) A. Quantity of the (implied) object

overeat, overbuy, overbuild, overpay, overcharge, oversell, overspend, overproduce, etc.

B. Extent of the action

overact, overdevelop, overdress, overwork, oversleep, overstate, etc.

C. Degree of the state

overbusy, overcareful, overripe, overmodest, overcrowded, overconfident, etc.

Although <u>-sugiru</u> and <u>over-</u> have very similar functions, they differ in several interesting points. First of all, while <u>-sugiru</u> is completely productive in attaching to verbs and adjectives, <u>over-</u> is only semi-productive. This suggests the syntactic nature of the former as opposed to the latter. Secondly, when we look at (25-34) and (41) and compare them in terms of the scope of these suffixes, we notice that the scope of over- is only a subset of that of -sugiru. Specifically, over- cannot cover the frequency of the action nor extend to the adverb, as shown below:

(42) a. Taroo wa warai-sugiru/ ziman-si-sugiru.
    TOP laugh-exces. boast-exces.
    'Taro laughs too often/ boasts too often.'

  b. ⁿ Taro overlaughs/ overboasts.

(43) a. Taroo wa hayaku tuki-sugi-ta.
    TOP early arrvie-exces.-PAST
    'Taro arrived too early.'

  b. ⁿ*Taro over-arrived early.

The absurdity of (43b) illustrates the third point, which is the most significant difference between over- and -sugiru. Namely, over- has a strong tendency to keep its scope limited to the word it attaches to, while -sugiru has no such restriction. This tendency of over- takes form as an interesting restriction it imposes on the possible arguments of the derived verb. The following contrast has been noted (Bresnan 1982a, Carlson and Roeper 1980):

(44) a. John overate.

  b. *John overate apples.

and has been used as evidence to claim that over- 'imposes intransitivity' (Carlson and Roeper 1980). In other words, eat must be 'intransitivized' by the object deletion rule (see Chapter II for some discussion) in order to combine with over-. Although this is an accurate description of (44), and the pattern generalizes to other verbs as well, (cf. overbid, overbuild, overspend, etc.) it does not exhaust the scope of this affix. Consider the following contrast:

(45) a. They overcharged *money / John.
 b. They overpaid *my salary / me.
 c. Mary overfeeds *milk to her son / her son.
 d. John overloaded *hay / the wagon.

The sentences in (45) can take an object NP, but it can be only one of the two options. The restriction here is not the transitivity of the derived verb, but rather that what is in the scope of over- (i.e., the entity which is 'excessive' in amount) cannot be expressed as an explicit argument but must be incorporated in the verb. The fact that the object is incorporated in (45a) is shown by the following sentence where the excessive amount can be specified in an adverbial phrase.

(46) They overcharged John by as much as $10.

Note, however, that this restriction is not an absolute one, but a few instances of over-V with an explicit object NP do exist:

(47) a. He was advised not to overbuy fertilizer.
 b. They overproduced / overstocked / oversupplied the merchandise.

What we are observing here can be stated as the conflict between different properties of this affix. Being a lexical affix, it cannot reach beyond the verb it attaches to, while its semantic function includes the object argument in its scope. This conflict is resolved when the particular verb can incorporate the object argument (as in 44a, 45), but the lexical restriction is loosened in a few cases where the object argument cannot be incorporated (as in 47). This strong tendency of over- to limit its scope to the lexical verb it attaches to is not found with -sugiru as we have seen above, which follows from its syntactic nature.

When a V' -sugiru construction with [-stative] feature is used as a predicate, it is sometimes nominalized and become a [+stative] predicate nominal. What is interesting about this predicate nominal formation is that although the head predicate is a nominal, the complements is not turned into a nominal modifier:

(48) Taroo wa [byooki ni nari]-sugi da.
     TOP   sick   become exces. COP
  'Taro becomes sick too often.'

(49) Taroo wa [osoku made kaisya de hataraki]-sugi da.
     TOP   late until office LOC work   exces. COP
  'Taro works in his office until too late.'

Here again, we have a case of phrasal suffixation resulting in a structure building. The configurations [Dative NP N] and [ADV N] are not generated by the PSR of Japanese. This predicate nominal form of V' -sugiru, in turn, supports our contention that the suffix attaches to a V' phrase.

This preservation of complements under predicate nominal formation with -sugi, however, does not extend to the regular nominalization of V'-sugiru, where the derived nominal is used as a case-marked NP. Observe the following examples:

(50) Hon no / *o yomi-sugi wa me ni warui.
    book GEN ACC read-exces.TOP eye DAT bad
    'Reading too many books is bad for the eyes.'

(51) Koozyoo de no / *de hataraki-sugi ga gen'in da.
    factory LOC GEN LOC wodk-exces. NOM cause COP
    'It is due to the overworking in the factory.'

The regular nominalization as exemplified above does not create structure but rather conforms to the NP structure of Japanese. We have seen in the previous section that the nominalization of V' -au also comforms to the NP structure.

These two types of nominal formation of V' -sugiru are quite suggestive of the ways in which the discrepancy between syntax and morphology in the phrasal suffixation is resolved (or not resolved). The predicate nominal formation is characteristic of the agglutinative verbal morphology exhibited in Japanese. Consider (48) again:

(48) Taroo wa [byooki ni nari]-sugi da.
         TOP sick DAT become exces. COP
    'Taro becomes sick too often.'

In this sentence the V' (in the bracket) by itself is well-formed, and the derived word nari-sugi is also well-formed. The fact that the whole predicate nominal phrase is not in accordance to the PSR of Japanese is somehow obscured (or backgrounded) by the well-formedness of the local combinatorics. On the other hand, in the regular nominalization it is the well-formedness of the NP structure as a whole that is maintained. Consider (50) again.

(50) a. [Hon o yomi]-sugiru.
        book ACC read exces. 'read too many books'

b. [hon no] [yomi-sugi]
      book GEN   read exces. 'reading too many books'

In (50a) -sugiru combines with a V'. When the resulting structure is an input for the nominalization, however, it is treated as a regular [NP V] structure in accordance with its word boundaries. As a result, (50b) does not preserve the V' constituent in the scope of -sugiru, but obeys the PSR for NP in Japanese. Hence this type of nominalization can be viewed as another instance of reanalysis over the phrasal suffixation structure (V'+suff. -> X V+suff.), which we examined in some detail in the preceding chapter with respect to alternating case markings.

It is significant that it is the predicate nominal formation that preserves the V' structure. Namely, predicate nominals share some properties with verbs in their semantic functions: with the help of a copula they appear either as a main predicate or as a modifier to a noun. They do not appear, on the other hand, in an argument position with a case marker. As we have discussed earlier, it is with the verbal morphology that the typical agglutinaive mode of concatenation is observed in Japanese. It is not surprising, then, that the predicate nominals but not the ordinary derived nominals exhibit the nominalization that incorporate a suffixed phrase. This point is significant because predicate nominal forming suffixes that can attach to a V' are rather common in Japanese, as shown in the following section.

2. Nominal forming suffixes

In this section we will give a survey of nominal forming suffixes which attach to a phrase. We will see that the pattern is especially productive with predicate nominal formation. In this type of suffixation some suffixes can attach to different types of V'.

Japanese has several nominal suffixes that attach to a V' phrase and form a predicate nominal. In terms of their semantic function, they are similar to adverbs, and the derived constructions are called 'adverbial nominals' in Martin (1977), where numerous examples of them are cited. These constructions have otherwise been given very little attention in the literature in the study of either morphology or syntax of Japanese. In the following, most commonly used nominal suffixes are exemplified.

2.1. Adjectival nominal forming suffixes

The difference between adjectival noun (AN) and noun (N) is that AN has an ending _na_ while N takes the genitive _no_ when used as a nominal modifier.

A. -gati (V'_) 'tend to V''

(52) [kare ga iru koto o wasure]-gati da.
　　　he NOM be COMO ACC forget tend COP
　　'(I) tend to forget that he is there.'

(53) [Dare nimo ari]-gati na ayamati
　　　anybody LOC be tend　　mistake
　　'a mistake that anybody tends to make'

Besides attaching to V''s, this suffix can idiosyncratically attach to some nouns: byooki-gati 'get sick often', huhei-gati 'complaint-ridden' rusu-gati 'being away often'.

  B. -ge (A'_) 'appears to be A''

   (54) [mono o ii-ta]-ge na me-tuki
         thingACC say-want-appear eye expression
        'eyes expressing the desire to talk'

In standard Japanese this suffix attachs only to A' (morphologically to the stem of the head adjective), but in the northern dialect (Toohoku dialect) the same morpheme is used as a sentence particle expressing the reportive style.

   (55) [umi e it-ta] ge na.
         sea GO goPAST PART 'I hear (he) went to the sea.'

Note that in this usage -ge follows the fully inflected form of the verb.

  C. -soo (A'_, V'_) 'appears to (be)'

This suffix is almost identical to -ge except that it can attach to V' as well. This morpheme can also appear with S (in standard Japanese unlike -ge) to express the fact that the proposition is hearsay. The following pair shows the contrast of its use as a suffix and a sentence particle (or an auxiliary).

   (56) a. Taroo wa [Tokyo e iki]-soo da.
              TOP   GO go appears COP
          'Taro appears to (soon) go to Tokyo.'

       b. Taroo wa [Tokyo e iku / itta] soo da.
          'I hear that Taro will go /went to Tokyo.'

Our contention that the suffixal use (56a) forms an AN predicate, while the sentence particle use (56b) does not is confirmed by the fact that the former can appear as a NP modifier, while the latter cannot.

(57) a. Tokyo e iki-soo na hito
          GO go appear   person
      'a person who appears to (soon) go to Tokyo'

    *Tokyo e iku soo na / no hito

The sentence particle use of -soo and -ge (54,55b) is not part of the morphological operation since it appears next to a fully inflected word, and hence is not within the scope of this study. However, the particles are clearly related to the suffixes, and demonstrate the varied structural domains certain morphemes in Japanese can cover in their domain.

Undoubtedly, the agglutinative morphology (especially of the verb) and the completely head-final configuration of the language contribute to this phenomenon. As a result, a verbal suffix can extend its scope to V', V'', and so on, without discontinuity in its domain (unlike the case of English).

2.2. Predicate nominal forming suffixes

Many of the predicate nominal forming suffixes convey aspectual meaning. One of their interesting characteristics is that when they can attach to a transitive V', and they modify the object NP, while when they attach to an intransitive V', they modify the subject NP.

A. -tate (V'_) 'freshly, newly (V'-ed)'

(58) [taki]-tate no gohan 'freshly cooked rice'
    cook newly GEN rice

(59) [piano o narai]-tate no kodomo
     pianoACC learn newly GEN child
     'a child who has just learned to play the piano'

B. -ppanasi (V'_) 'leave x V-d'

(60) [terebi o tuke]-ppanasi da.
     TV   ACC turn on leave COP
     '(We) have left the TV set on.'

An alternative case marking possibility for (60), shown below, indicates that this aspectual suffix can be interpreted as attaching only to V, just as we saw with -te aru 'has already been' in Chapter IV.

(61) Terebi ga [tuke]-ppanasi da.
     TV   NOM turn on leave COP
     'The TV set has been left on.'

C. -kake 'be about to'

(62) [byooki ga naori]-kake no kodomo
     illness NOM heal about to child
     'a child who is recovering from an illness'

(63) [yomi]-kake no hon
     read about to book
     'a book that (I'm) in the middle of reading'

This suffix is a nominalized form of the verbal suffix -kakeru.

(64) [hon o yomi]-kakeru.
     book ACC read start 'start reading a book.'

D. -doosi 'keep on V-ing'

(65) Taroo wa [hahaoya ni sikar-are]-doosi da.
     TOP   mother DAT scoldPASS keep on COP
     'Taro is always scolded by his mother.'

This suffix also has a verbal suffix form: -toosu. Note that we find rendaku, which applies only within a complex word but not in a phrase, on this nominal suffix. (See Chapter II Section 4 for the discussion on rendaku.)

E. -kkiri 'has V-ed and has done nothing else'

(66) Kare wa [heya ni hairi]-kkiri da.
    he TOP room LOC enter   COP
    'He has gone into the room (and has not come out).'

The same morpheme can attach to S and follow an inflected V.[2]

(67) Konsyuu wa [hon o issatu yon-da] kiri da.
    this week TP book ACC one readPAST   COP
    '(I have) read just one book this week
    and nothing else.'

Let us summarize here the common characteristics of the nominal forming suffixes that we have seen here. They attach to V' in a way parallel to that of verbal suffixes, and they nominalize the predicate as a whole. The fact that they are closely related to the phrasal verbal suffixes can be seen by the large number of them having a verbal form as well. Another noteworthy point about these suffixes is the fact that some of them can attach to a V' and S (not necessarily as a suffix). Also, even though they basically attach to V''s, some instances of them are restructured as attaching only to V. As has been mentioned earlier, this flexibility in the domain of suffixation is one of the vital characteristics of Japanese verbal morphology.

---

[2]The gemination of the consonant in -kkiri indicates the presence of a glottal stop. Note that when it attaches to S in (67) there is no glottal stop. The same phonological feature is observed with -ppanasi (cf. 60), whose base form is -hanasi (derived from a verb hanasu 'to let free'). This phonological change is quite similar to rendaku in many respects.

3. Subordinate clause suffixes

There are a number of morphemes in Japanese which attach to an infinitival form of a verb in a clause and make the whole clause subordinate. They express a temporal relation of some sort between the main clause and the subordinate clause. Some of them are cited in Kageyama (1982), and a large number of them can be found in Martin (1975). Some examples are listed below:

(68) Taroo wa [uta o utai]-nagara aruite kita.
       TOP songACC sing while walk comePAST
'Taro came walking, while singing songs.'

(69) [Kooen o sanpo si]-gatera . . .
    park ACC walk do while
'while taking a walk in the park..'

(70) Taroo wa [soba o toori]-sina ni aisatu-si-ta.
       TOP near ACC pass when greet do PAST
'Taro greeted me as he passed by.'

As shown by these examples many of them require the subordinate subject to be null and coreferential to the subject NP of the main clause.[3]

---

[3]A different type of morphological operation that is quite similar to (68)-(80) in its function and property is the reduplication on V to express 'while V-ing'. (68) above can be paraphrased as:
(i) Taroo wa uta o utai-utai aruite kita.
     TOP song sing walk came
'Taro came walking, singing songs.'
Reduplication is quite a productive operation in Japanese morphology, and it has many functions; reduplicated N expresses plurality, reduplicated A expresses 'very A', and so on. But the type of verb reduplication mentioned here seems to be the most 'syntactic' of them.

The suffix -nagara has another use in which it attaches to a clause with an independent subject NP and functions as a conjunction marker with the meaning 'even though'.

(71) [Sensei ga soba ni i]-nagara seito ga oboreta.
    teacher NOM near LOC be though student drowned
    'A student got drowned, although a teacher was nearby.'

This example is also suggestive of the ways in which a suffix in Japanese can have different domains with different semantic functons.[4]

As we have mentioned, Kageyama (1982) cites some of the nominal forming suffixes we saw in Section 2 and the subordinate forming suffixes we just saw in this section. After pointing out that they are word formation processes that involve a phrasal unit, he suggests two ways of handling them. First, for the nominal forming suffixes Kageyama suggests that there should be a limited recursion from syntax to morphology, which, he states, 'although . . . is no doubt a weakening of the [autonomous] morphological theory, it will be admitted as a well-defined constrained weakening in that the recursion applies only to a handful of specific constructions.' In other words, he suggests that this type of phrasal suffixation is a marked phenomenon particular to a few idiosyncratic expressions. On the other hand, for the subordination suffixes Kageyama suggests a

---

[4]Note that this dual function of -nagara is quite similar to _while_ in English, except that -nagara as a temporal subordinator requires a null subject and English _while_ in the temporal sense does not have this restriction.

phonological readjustment rule by which a bound conjunct is lowered into the S and phonologically attached to the infinitive verb. This way, he states, the lexicalist assumption (i.e., no phrasal unit allowed in the morphology) is maintained.

There are several questions that immediately come up, which are not discussed by Kagayama. (He states these proposals as programmatic ones and does not discuss them in great detail.) First of all, given these two options to handle the violations of the lexicalist hypothesis, how do we decide which case should be a recursion from syntax to morphology and which case should be a phonological readjustment? Do we need both mechanisms? Are they really well-constrained enough so that the lexicalist hypothesis can be maintained in the face of them?

In the approach taken in this study, where the interaction of phrasal operation and morphological operation is allowed when they belong to the same type of rules (syntactic or lexical), it is natural to consider the various sort of predicate-nominal forming suffixes we discussed in Section 2 as instances of phrasal suffixation. They are completely productive and semantically compositional, which indicates their syntactic nature, and yet they involve a category change parallel in form to an ordinary morphological derivation; a suffix attaches to the stem (or infinitive) form of the predicate and the output belongs to the same lexical category as that of the suffix, i.e., the head element. In these respects they are parallel to such phrasal suffixation cases as the V'-tai construction discussed in Chapter III and IV. We have also observed that this type of nominal formation on the V' unit is rather common in the predicate position, and that a number of predicate nominal forming suffixes have verbal counterparts. (See Section 1.2. for the discussion on the difference between the regular nominalization and the predicate nominal formation of V'-sugiru.) Given all these considerations it is difficult to maintain the lexicalist assumption and treat these cases of phrasal suffixation as exceptional in the morphology of Japanese, as suggested by Kageyama (1982). Rather, it seems natural to admit the phrasal scope of the various suffixes (especially verbal) in Japanese, and give them the systematic treatment that they deserve.

Turning to the subordinate-clause forming suffixes, we notice that they appear to be different from the predicate-nominal forming suffixes in the following ways: While it is clear that the predicate nominal forming suffixes are lexically N (many of them are formally nominalized verbs), it is not clear with the subordinate-forming suffixes whether they belong to a certain lexical category or even whether they should be the head of the constituent. Consider (67) again:

(67) Taroo wa [uta o uati]-nagara aruite kita.
'Taro came walking, singing songs.'

Suppose the subordinate clause is lexically an adverbial, which is not implausible, given its function as a temporal modifier to the main clause. Can we say that -nagara is an adverbial suffix? Is it plausible to consider it as the head of the constituent in the same way a nominalizing suffix determines the category of the phrase? Actually, there is some evidence suggesting that -nagara is not the lexical head of the constituent in the usual sense. V'nagara can be a nominal modifier taking the genitive marker, which indicates that the constituent as a whole belongs to the category of N.

(72) [uta o utai-nagara] no sanpo
     'a walk while singing songs'

Hence the use of this constituent as a subordinate clause does not follow from its lexical category, but must be specified with the suffix, in the same way many subordinate markers (such as kara 'after, because') are specified as attaching syntactically to S. In these respects it is difficult to consider the suffixation of -nagara to be an ordinary morphological derivation.

It then seems that there is some plausibility in treating the subordinate forming suffixes as a case of cliticization, i.e., a postsyntactic phonological adjustment, as suggested by Kageyama (1982). Suppose the fact that such suffix as -nagara in (67) is attached to V as a bound morpheme has no reality in syntax or morphology but only in phonology. Then it is not a problem any more that it does not lexically head the phrase nor participate in morphological derivation, or that it has the syntactic function of subordinating the clause it attaches to. We have earlier discussed cliticization in relation to our rule typology scheme, and questioned how it can be distinguished from phrasal suffixation (cf. Chapter I, Section 3.4.). We can now say that phrasal suffixation belongs to the derivational morphological system while cliticizaion does not. Thus if the process in consideration has the properties of belonging to derivational morphology, namely, the head determining the category of the output, the derivation following the morphological rules in form, and so on, it should be considered as a suffixation process rather than cliticization. On the other hand, if the suffixation does not have any characteristics of belonging to derivational morphology, it should be treated as cliticization. Consequently, in our approach, cliticization is not a principled interaction of morphology and syntax, while phrasal suffixation is. Note that the lexicalist hypothesis cannot make this distinction but rather rules out both types of processes as being exceptional.[5]

---

[5]Pranka (1983) proposes two types of word formation fed by syntax; merger and fusion. Merger forms a complex word (examples are taken from Papago V-Aux merger) that belongs to the lexical category of the head, while fusion (examples are from Romance Preposition-Article fusion) does not produce an item that belongs to a lexical category. While this distinction is similar to the one we make between phrasal suffixation and cliticization, Pranka does not treat merger as part of word formation, and does not comment on

Let us summarize our findings so far. We have contended that the verbal suffixation with a phrasal scope is not a marked process in Japanese morphology. The difference between Japanese and English in this respect was discussed with the affixes -sugiru and over-. We have then observed that the predicate position allows phrasal nominalization as opposed to the regular nominal position. The productivity of the predicate nominal formation and its parallelism to ordinary word-level derivational morphology lead us to believe that they should not be treated as an exceptional recursion from syntax to morphology but rather as a case of systematic interaction between phrasal and morphological operation. Finally it was pointed out that subordinate clause forming suffixes are special in that they do not seem to lexically head the constituent, and that their attachment should justifiably be treated as phonological readjustment rather than part of derivational morphology.

4. The domain of passive suffixation

We have observed in this chapter that verbal suffixes in Japanese are quite flexible in the domains they attach to. It will be argued in this section that the passive suffix -rare also has multiple domains of suffixation and that the proposed analysis can naturally account for some facts about Passive that must otherwise be stipulated.

---

how general the phenomena can be.

It has been held by many that the passive formation in English applies in two places of the grammar: the lexicon and syntax. Wasow (1977) has given convincing arguments that adjectival passives are formed in the lexicon, while regular passives are derived in syntax.[6] As for the domain of syntactic passives, it was argued by Keenan (1981) that the domain of application is phrasal (TVP in his terms) and not sentential. (Readers are referred to these works for details.) We just assume here that the domains of passive morphology in English are V (for adjectival passives) and V' (for syntactic passives).

Passivization is probably the most studied topic in the generative syntax of Japanese. One major controversy remains, however, concerning the deep structure of the two types of passives that exist in Japanese. In addition to the regular passive that is parallel to the English syntactic passive such as (73), there is another type of passive, called 'adversative passive', which has no analog in English (cf. 74).

(73) Taroo wa sensei ni sikar-are-ta.
     TOP teacher DAT scold-PASS-PAST
    'Taro was scolded by his teacher.'

(74) Taroo wa chichi ni sin-are-ta.
     TOP father DAT die-PASS-PAST
    'Taro's father died (on him).'

---

[6]For the claim that all passive formations are lexical, see Bresnan (1982a).

In the transformational approach to passive, it has been agreed that the adversative passive involves a sentence embedding in the deep structure:

(75)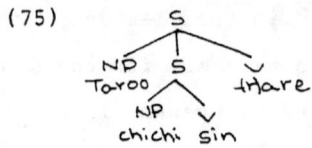

On the other hand, there have been basically two approaches to the regular passive. One approach (the non-uniform theory) assigns the deep structure without sentence embedding (76a); the other (the uniform theory) assigns the same structure to both passives (76b).

(76) a.   b.
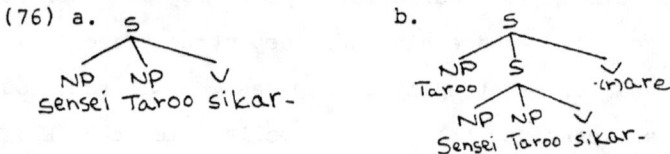

The controversy has involved many complex arguments based mainly on the interaction of passive with other syntactic rules such as reflexivization. (See Kuno 1978 and the references cited there.) As Kuno (1978) notes, the arguments for these two positions seem to have been exhausted without giving a clear answer as to which position should be taken.[7]

---

[7] Kuno (1983) rejects his previous non-uniform theory and proposes a uniform theory approach augmented by some principles that involve the notion 'degree of adversity.'

In the transformational approach to passive formations, the suffix -rare has been postulated either as a main verb in the deep structure for the structure (76b) or as being inserted by the transformation to the structure (76a). Morphologically speaking, however, -rare is a bound suffix that attaches to V, and since it is a verbal suffix, it is quite possible that its scope extends beyond the word level. In fact, it is quite plausible to consider the regular passive formation as the suffixation on V' parallel to the analysis proposed by Keenan (1980) for English syntactic passives. Consider the following:

(77) a. Taroo wa Hanako o yuusyoku ni yon-da.
         TOP   ACC dinner DAT invite-PAST
    'Taro invited Hanako for dinner.'

   b. Hanako wa Taroo ni [yuusyoku ni yob]-are-ta.
         TOP   DAT   dinner DAT invite-PASS-PAST
    'Hanako was invited for dinner by Taro.'

(78) a. Taroo wa Hanako no waruguti o it-ta.
         TOP   GEN bad words ACC say-PAST
    'Taro spoke ill of Hanako.'

   b. Hanako wa Taroo ni [waruguti o iw]-are-ta.
         TOP   DAT bad words ACC say-PASS-PAST
    'Hanako was spoken ill of by Taro.'

It is natural to consider that the bracketed constituents (V') are in the scope of -rare just as the verb -sikar- in (73) is.[8]

---

[8] Examples such as (78b) have been analyzed as adversative passives because the derived subject is not either direct or indirect object in the active sentence. It was argued earlier in this chapter, however, that the bracketed V' in (78b) should be analyzed as a complex transitive predicate in view of the suffixation of the reciprocal suffix -au. (See Section 1.1.)

Should we then contend that <u>-rare</u> is a V' suffix? There is some evidence of a morphological nature which indicate that for the regular passive, <u>-rare</u> cannot extend beyond the V' level. Note that aspectual markers cannot precede <u>-rare</u> but must follow it.

(79) a. Taroo wa Hanako o mitume-te i-ta.
          TOP   ACC watch   PROG-PAST
    'Taro was watching Hanako.'

    b. Hanako wa Taroo ni mitume-rare-te i-ta.
          TOP   DAT   watch-PASS-PROG-PAST
    'Hanako was being watched by Taro.'

    c. *Hanako wa Taroo ni mitume-te i-rare-ta.
    '*Hanako was be-watching-ed by Taro.'

(80) a. Taroo wa Hanako o nikumi-dasi-ta.
          TOP   ACC hate-begin-PAST
    'Taro began to hate Hanako.'

    b. Hanako wa Taroo ni nikum-are-dasi-ta.
          TOP   DAT   hate-PASS-begin-PAST
    'Hanako began to be hated by Taro.'

    c. *Hanako wa Taroo ni nikumi-das-are-ta.
    '*Hanako was begin-to-hated by Taro.'

These data automatically follow if we assume that the aspectual markers combine with V' and constitute V'', and postulate that the scope of <u>-rare</u> is limited to V'.

Note that the same restrictions apply to English passives, as the ungrammaticality of the translations for (79c) and (80c) shows. McCawley (1980) accounts for this phenomena by pointing out that Passive can apply only to the 'lowest' S (in his framework Aux's are main verbs), since it is the only S where the condition for Passive is met. In an alternative framework where the passive formation is phrasal, the same result can be achieved by restricting the domain to V', with the assumption that Aux and V' constitute V''.

Turning to the other kind of passive in Japanese, we find some striking data, which indicates that the situation with the adversative passive is the opposite. Various aspectual markers can occur before the passive suffix, as shown below:

(81) Taroo wa Hanako ni yodoosi oki-te i-rare-ta.
          TOP   DAT all night stay up-PROG-PASS-PAST
     'Hanako stayed up all night (on Taro).'

(82) Taroo wa Hanako ni tooku e it-te simaw-are-ta.
          TOP   DAT far GO go PERF   PASS-PAST
     'Hanako has gone to far away (to Taro's sorrow.)'

(83) Uma ni totuzen hasiri-das-arete . . .
     horse DAT suddenly run-begin-PASS
     'The horse suddenly started to run (to my surprise)'

(84) Hanako ni zutto syaberi-tuzuke-rare-ta.
            DAT continuously talk-continue-PASS-PAST
     'Hanako kept talking (to me) endlessly.'

These data can be accounted for if we allow <u>-rare</u> to attach beyond the V' level. Note that for the uniform theory, the difference between the regular passive and the adversative passive must be stipulated in some way so that for the regular passive the embedded S cannot include Aux. For the non-uniform theory, on the other hand, this set of data can be used as a strong piece of evidence for having an embedded S only for the adversative passive.[9]

---

[9] It is raher puzzling that this type of data has not been discussed (in the literature I have seen), especially by the supporters of the non-uniform theory. It is conceivable, however, that viewing <u>-rare</u> as a main verb has kept people from examining its morphological domain as a suffix.

Consequently, we propose that the passive -rare has two domains of suffixation: the regular -rare attaches to V' and the adversative -rare attaches to V''. Note that even though the non-uniform theory can make the similar distinction, -rare is given there two completely different sources. The regular passive suffix does not exist in the deep structure but is inserted with the passive transformaion, while the adversative passive is in the deep structure as a main verb. Our proposed analysis has the advantage of treating both instances of -rare uniformally as a verbal suffix differing only in the domain it attaches to. We have already seen that it is not unusual in the Japanese verbal morphology that one suffix has multiple domains. Note further that the lexicalist approach to the passive suffixation (Farmer 1980, Miyagawa 1980) cannot deal with the data presented here, since the suffix can only attach to V in their framework.

The question arises here as to whether the adversative passive -rare must subcategorize for S at a 'deeper level' in syntax, given the fact that the dative-marked NP is the subject of the V'' to which -rare attaches. Actually, there is also evidence that the embedded S must exist as a domain of the honorification (triggered by the subject NP) before the passive suffixation applies. It has been noted that some cases of adversative passive can have honorification marker inside the passive suffix, although this is not very common.[10]

(85) Soo nanimokamo o-mitoosi ni nar-are-te wa . . .
such everything   understand HONO-PASS-
'Since you understand absolutely everything
(to my dismay) . . .'

This is totally impossible for the regular passive:

(86) *Kodomo wa Tennoo ni o-home ni nar-are-ta.
child TOP emperor DAT praise HONO-PASS-PAST
'The child was praised by the emperor.'

Thus it is plausible to assume that the adverative passive has an embedded S in the deep structure, and that the passive operation raises the subject NP and marks it with the dative case, while attaching -rare to the V'' node that is left. We will not go into the syntactic details of the passive formation, which is beyond the scope of this study. Our point here is that the domain of suffixation must be regarded as different between the regular passive (V') and the adversative passive (V''), when the suffixation takes place.

As for the passive suffixation on the lexical level, it has been pointed out (see Jacobson 1980) that the passive suffix is intricately involved in the transitivity paradigm of Japanese verbal morphology. In addition, the morpheme -(r)ar(e) figures in some cases of potential formation, as well as in one type of honorification marker, which can very well be historically related. To take one example, consider

---

[10]The examples of this sort have been given in Kuno (1983:65) as a counterexample to the lexicalist approach to Passive. It seems that they are more acceptable if it is the addressee that is honorified.

the pair <u>umu</u> 'give birth to' and <u>umareru</u> 'be born'. The latter is the passive form of the former, but <u>umareru</u> has been lexicalized as an intransitive verb, and hence it can occur with syntactic passive formation:

(86) Nikagetu mo hayaku akanboo ni umare-rare-ta.
    two months early   baby DAT be born-PASS-PAST
    '(My) baby was born as much as two months too early.'

Miyagawa (1980) discusses the lexicalization of causative-suffixed verbs in detail. We have also seen in this study that many syntactic word formations can undergo lexicalization.

We have argued in this section that Japanese passive -<u>rare</u> has two different phrasal domains of suffixation, V' for the regular passive and V'' for the adversative passive, in addition to the lexical level of V. Thus the passive morphology in English and Japanese differ only in that the latter has V'' as a possible domain. This difference is in accordance with our other observations made earlier that Japanese verbal suffixes are much more flexible in extending domains beyond the level of V, compared with English.

CHAPTER VI
CONCLUDING REMARKS

This study started out with a survey of major issues in the recent works on word formation, many of which adhere to the lexicalist hypothesis, which maintains that word formation belongs solely to the lexicon and does not interact with syntax. This position has in the recent years been particularly popular for derivational morphology, although it has been challenged in regard to inflectional morphology in works such as Anderson (1982) and more recently Carlson (1983). I have argued in this study, however, that the lexicalist assumption cannot be maintained for derivational morphology as well.

An alternative approach was outlined in Chapter I, in which rule type (syntactic/lexical) is a separate dimension from domain of operation (phrasal /morphological), which allows for syntactic rules with morphological operations and lexical rules with phrasal operations. These two types of rules have been a problem to the lexicalist view, and when acknowledged, have been claimed to constitute marked exceptions to the grammar. It has been argued, however, that those processes should rather be treated as principled interaction of syntax and the lexicon, as well as phrase structure rules and word formation rules. It has been shown that with this approach some significant generalizations can be captured.

One major prediction of the proposed rule typology is that the interaction of PSR and WFR is possible only when they belong to the same type of rule (syntactic/lexical). When a morphological operation is syntactic, it can in principle apply to a syntactically generated phrase, since the process is productive and semantically compositional. On the other hand, a lexical word formation, being idiosyncratic by nature, cannot have a freely generated phrase as input, and when it appears to apply to a phrasal unit, that unit actually is a product of a lexical rule with phrasal operation (called 'lexical unit formation' here). In this respect we have discussed in Chapter I the contrast between _heard of_ which can undergo _un_-prefixation (_unheard-of_) because it has been lexicalized as an A, and _heard about_, which is not lexicalized and hence cannot be input for a lexical word formation (cf. *_unheard about_). Such occurrences of a phrasal lexical unit in some complex words have been noted in the lexicalist works (e.g., Kiparsky 1983), and have been treated as an exceptional recursion from syntax to morphology. If indeed only a lexicalized phrase could be found in a complex word, the 'limited recursion' view makes sense. It has been argued in Chapter II, however, that English verbal compounding and complex adjective formation have a syntactically generated phrase as input. If these processes must also be treated as a recursion from syntax to morphology, then the productivity and the semantic transparency of the processes undermine the fundamental claim of the lexicalist hypothesis that there is no systematic and productive interaction of syntax and morphology.

Consequently, it is the existence of syntactic rules with morphological operation, which in principle allows a freely generated phrase to be input to word formation, that poses a serious threat to the lexicalist hypothesis. In English derivational morphology, as shown in Chapter II, only a few suffxies (V'+er, V'+ing, V'+ed, N'+ed) belong to this category. In Japanese, where verbal morphology exhibits a typical agglutinative mode of concatenation, however, a large number of suffixes were shown in the remaining chapters to have a phrasal scope. In Chapter II the agent nominal forming suffix -te was argued to be syntactic, as opposed to the agent nominal compound formation. In Chapter III two nominalizing suffixes on adjective -sa and -mi were discussed and the former was shown to be syntactic, as opposed to the latter. It was further observed that even though -sa by itself does not attach to a phrase, its complete productivity allows it to apply to the phrasal adjectival suffixes, -tai 'want to' and -yasui 'easily'. This is a typical case of interaction between PSR (V' formation) and WFR (suffixation), made possible by the syntactic nature of both.

One particularly interesting consequences of allowing phrasal suffixation is that the process can create a structure not generated by PSR. In Chapter IV, a V'-suffix -tai along with other stative predicate forming suffixes were discussed, and it was claimed that some instances of V'+suffix are actually reanalyzed as [X] [V+suffix]. This assumption was then shown to give a natural account for some facts concerning the alternating case markings on X, which problem has attracted competing analyses in the recent years. In Chapter V, a variety of V'-suffixes were discussed, and it was observed that some of them have multiple domains (V', V'', S, etc.). This particular assumption about the domains of suffixation led to a natural account regarding the difference between the two types of Passives in Japanese in terms of their morphological restrictions, which cannot follow from either a lexicalist analysis or a transformational analysis on passives. Thus it was demonstrated that allowing phrasal suffixation not only gives a plausible description of various constructions involved, but also provides a motivated account for the syntactic and morphological facts about them.

Aside from the claims about the rule typology, we have made some observations on the principles that governs various word formation processes. One salient factor that was found to be regulating many facts about compound formation and nominalization of V and A is argument structure, which plays a crucial role in syntax as well. In Chapter II it was argued that one difference between Japanese and English is the lack of the lexical intransitivization rule in the former, and that this difference is reflected in the types of deverbal nominal compounds of these languages. In Chapter III it was shown that in the nominalization of adjectives in both Japanese and English, there is a hierarchy of thematic roles in what can occupy the genitive subject position. This fact, along with the complete productivity of the nominalization suffix -sa yielded some clarification for the problems surrounding 'two-place' adjective constructions in Japanese in terms of their case markings and constituent structures.

On the other hand, one principle that was shown to be applying only in word formation is what is called 'the generic condition' in Chapter II. In addition to the well-known fact that compounds in general contain only generic nouns, we have observed the same condition to be applying to the lexical unit formation of such complex adjectives as easy-to-clean, lovely-to-look-at, which provided an explanation for why the same rule cannot apply to eager to please.

I have started this study hoping to extend the programmatic proposal for the rule typology made by Dowty

(1979). Even though this approach has proven to be quite fruitful in shedding light to the interaction of morphology and syntax across typologically different languages, there are many areas of inquiry left for future research. For instance, we have seen that English is quite limited in syntactic suffixation, and hence a productive type of interaction of syntax and morphology is accordingly limited. On the other hand, English seems to allow the other type of interaction, namely, the lexical unit formation feeding word formation. We have seen some properties of this procces; that it applies to the surface sequence of some sort, obeys the generic condition, and that the output is a semantic constituent that seems to be limited to the category V or A. There have been studies on relevant phenomena (e.g., Hornstein and Weinberg 1981, Carlson and Roeper 1981, various works in LFG by Bresnan, etc.), but it is clear that we are far from fully understanding the nature and scope of this process. The predicted properties of the lexical unit formation must be further investigated against more data, and examined in terms their consequences on the theory of syntax and morphology.

As for phrasal suffixation processes, even though a large part of this work was devoted to their discussion, many issues are left unresolved. There seems to be a sharp contrast in Japanese between nominal morphology, which rarely extends beyond a word level, and verbal morphology, which was shown to be quite flexible in its scope. This contrast must be given a principled explanation. Further, a problem remains as to what is the proper distinction of levels (V, V', V'', etc.) as the domains of phrasal suffixation. In any case, as was demonstrated for the analysis of stative predicate constructions and passives, the pursuit of this particular approach will quite likely yield new perspectives on the existing issues in Japanese syntax.

One major purpose of this work has been to propose an alternative theory to the recently popular lexicalist positions that are surveyed in Chapter I. While this study was underway, more works have appeared on the same issue. Sadock (1984) proposes an 'Autolexical Syntax' framework, which allows straightforward accounts for cliticization and noun incorporation by separating the phrase structure representation from the morphological structure representation. Although this approach shares one thing with the proposal made in this study, namely that the morphological operation can have a syntactic/semantic scope of phrasal level, they differ in one crucial point. In Autolexical Syntax the morphological structure is not semantically compositional, but only the syntactic structure is; we maintain both of them to be so. Thus we have argued that cliticization is not a principled interaction of morphology and syntax while phrasal suffixation is. In

Autolexical Syntax both are given the same treatment. I have not been able to evaluate the different consequences of the two positions and must leave it for future consideration. Other recent works of relevance (all happen to be in GB framework) include Pranka (1983), which proposes feedback from syntax to word formation at two different places in grammar (cf. Chapter V, fn. 5), Roeper and Keyser (1984), which proposes transformation and projection principle to be present in both the lexicon and syntax, and Borer (1984), which allows certain morphology to take place in syntax. There is no doubt that the lexicon/syntax boundary will continue to be one controversial and fruitful area of investigation in the study of natural languages.

BIBLIOGRAPHY

Abe, Yasuaki. 1981a. On the representation of argument structure. Proceedings of NELS 12.1-15. Amherst, Mass.: GLSA, University of Massachusetts.

----------. 1981b. Remarks on causativization. ms. University of Massachusetts.

Allen, Margaret. 1978. Morphological Investigations. Ph. D. dissertation. University of Connecticut.

Amritavalli, R. 1980. Expressing cross-categorial selectional correspondences: an alternative to the X' syntax approach. Linguistic Analysis 6.305-343.

Anderson, Stephen, R. 1977. Comments on the paper by Wasow. Formal Syntax. ed. by P. Cullicover et al. New York: Academic Press.

----------. 1982. Where's morphology? Linguistic Inquiry 13.571-612.

Aronoff, Mark. 1976. Word Formation in Generative Grammar. (LI Monograph 1.) Cambridge, Mass.: MIT Press.

Aronoff, M. and Sridhar, S. N. 1983. Morphological levels in English and Kannada. CLS Parasession on Interplay of Phonology, Morphology, and Syntax. Chicago: Chicago Linguistic Society.

Bloomfield, Leonard. 1933. Language. New York: H. Holt and Co.

Borer, Hagit. 1984. The projection principle and rules of morphology. Proceedings of NELS 14.16-33. Amherst, Mass.: GLSA, University of Massachusetts.

Bresnan, Joan, W. 1978. A realistic transformational grammar. Linguistic Theory and Psychological Reality, ed. by M. Halle, et al. Cambridge, Mass.: MIT Press.

----------. 1982a. Passive in lexical theory. The Mental Representation of Grammatical Relations, ed. by J. Bresnan. Cambridge, Mass.: MIT Press.

Bresnan, Joan, W. 1982b. Polyadicity. The Mental
Representation of Grammatical Relations, ed. by J.
Bresnan. Cambridge, Mass.: MIT Press.

Carlson, Gregory. 1983. Marking consituents. Linguistic
Categories: Auxiliaries and Related Puzzles, Vol. I,
ed. by F. Heny and B. Richards. Dordrecht: Reidel.

Carlson, G. and Roeper, T. 1980. Morphology and
subcategorization: case and the unmarked complex verb.
Lexical Grammar. ed. by T. Hoekstra, et al.
Dordrecht: Foris.

Chomsky, Noam A. 1972. Remarks on nominalization. Studies
on Semantics in Generative Grammar. The Hague: Mouton.

----------. 1981. Lectures on Government and Binding.
Dordrecht: Foris.

Downing, Pamela. 1978. On the creation and use of compounds
in English. Language 53.810-842.

Dowty, David. 1978. Governed transformations as lexical
rules in Montague Grammar. Linguistic Inquiry
9.393-427.

----------. 1979. Word Meaning and Montague Grammar.
Dordrecht: Reidel.

Farmer, Ann K. 1980. Interaction of Morphology and Syntax.
Ph. D. dissertation. MIT.

Fronek, Josef. 1982. 'Thing' as a function word.
Linguistics 20.633-654.

Haig, John. 1979. Real and apparent multiple subject
sentences. Papers in Japanese Linguistics 6.87-131.

Halle, Morris. 1973. Prolegomena to a theory of word
formation. Linguistic Inquiry 4.3-16.

Hasegawa, Nobuko. 1980. VP constituent in Japanese.
Linguistic Analysis 6.115-130.

Hoekstra, T. H., van der Hulst, and Moortgat, M. 1980.
Introduction. Lexical Grammar. ed. by T. Hoekstra, et
al. Dordrecht: Foris.

Hornstein, N and Weinberg, A. 1982. Case theory and
preposition stranding. Linguistic Inquiry 12.55-92.

Inoue, Kazuko. 1976. Henkei-bunpoo to Nihongo. Tokyo:
Taisyuukan.

Inoue, Kazuko.. 1979. 'Tough sentences' in Japanese. *Problems in Japanese Syntax and Semantics*, ed. by J. Hinds and I. Howard. Tokyo: Kaitakusya.

Jackendoff, Ray. 1972. *Semantic Interpretation in Generative Grammar*. Cambridge, Mass.: MIT Press.

----------. 1975. Morphological and semantic regularities in the lexicon. *Language* 51.639-671.

Jacobsen, Wesley. 1980. Transitivity in Japanese Verbal System. Ph. D. dissertation. University of Chicago.

Kageyama, Taro. 1980. *Goi no Koozoo: Niti-Ei Hikaku*. Tokyo: Syoohakusya.

----------. 1982. Word formation in Japanese. *Lingua* 57.215-258.

Keenan, Edward. 1980. Passive is phrasal (not sentential or lexical). *Lexical Grammar* ed. by T. Hoekstra, et al. Dordrecht: Foris.

Keyser, S. and Roeper, T. 1982. On middle verbs in English. ms. MIT/University of Massachusetts.

Kiparsky, Paul. 1982. Lexical Morphology and Phonology. *Linguistics in the Morning Calm*, ed. by the Linguistic Society of Korea, 3-91. Seoul: Hanshin Publishing Co.

----------. 1983. Word formation and the lexicon. to appear in *Proceeding of the 1982 Mid-America Linguistic Conference*. ed. by F. Ingeman. Lawrence: University of Kansas.

Kitahara, Yasuo. 1970. Zyodoosi no soogo-syoosetu ni tuite no koobunron-teki koosatu. *Kokugogaku* 83.32-59.

Kuno, Susumu. 1973. *The Structure of the Japanese Language*. Cambridge, Mass.: MIT Press.

----------. 1978. Theoretical perspectives on Japanese linguistics. *Problems in Japanese Syntax and Semantics*, ed. by J. Hinds and I. Howard. Tokyo: Kaitakusha.

----------. 1983. *Sin Bunpoo Kenkyuu*. Tokyo: Taisyuukan.

Kuroda, Shige-Yuki. 1978. Case marking, canonical sentence patterns, and counter equi in Japanese. *Problems in Japanese Syntax and Semantics*, ed. by J. Hinds and I. Howard. Tokyo: Kaitakusha.

Kuroda, S-Y. 1980. Bun no koozoo. *Niti-Ei hikaku kooza*. ed. by T. Kunihiro. Tokyo: Taishukan.

---------- 1981a. Some recent issues in linguistic theory and Japanese syntax. *Coyote Papers in Linguistics* 2.103-120. University of Arizona.

----------. 1981b. The biautonomy of syntax. *Linguistic Notes from La Jolla* 9.64-78. UC San Diego.

----------. 1983. What can Japanese say about government and binding? *Proceedings of West Coast Conference on Formal Linguistics* 2.153-164.

Lapointe, Steven, G. 1983. A comparison of two recent theories of agreement. *CLS Parasession on Interplay of Phonology, Morphology, and Syntax*. Chicago: CLS.

Lasnik, H. and Fiengo, R. 1974. Complement object deletion. *Linguistic Inquiry* 5.535-572.

Lees, Robert B. 1960. *The Grammar of English Nominalization*. The Hague: Mouton.

Lehr, Rachel. 1980. Persion nominalization and the source of complex nominals. *Proceedings of CLS* 16.192-222.

Levi, Judith. 1978. *The Syntax and Semantics of Complex Nominals*. New York: Academic Press.

Lieber, Rochelle. 1981. On the Organization of the Lexicon. Ph. D. dissertation. MIT.

----------. 1983. Argument linking and English compounds. *Linguistic Inquiry* 13.251-285.

Lipka, Leonhard. 1975. Re-discovery procedures and the lexicon. *Lingua* 37.197-224.

Maling, J. 1980. Transitive adjectives: a case of categorial reanalysis. ms. Brandeis University.

McCawley, James D. 1975. Review of Chomsky (1972). *Studies in English Linguistics* 3.209-311. Tokyo: Asahi Syuppan.

----------. 1981. An un-syntax. *Current Appproaches to Syntax* (Syntax and Semantics 13.), ed. by E. Moravcsik and J. Wirth. New York: Academic Press.

----------. 1982. The non-existence of syntactic categories. *Thirty Million Theories on Grammar*. Chicago: University of Chicago Press.

Makino, Seiichi. 1976. Nominal compounds. <u>Japanese</u>
<u>Generative</u> <u>Grammar</u> (Syntax and Semantics 5.), ed. by M.
Shibatani. New York: Academic Press.

Martin, Samuel. 1952. Morphophonemics of standard
colloquial Japanese. Supplement to <u>Language</u> 47.

----------. 1975. <u>A</u> <u>Reference</u> <u>Grammar</u> <u>of</u> <u>Japanese</u>. New
Haven: Yale University Press.

Miyagawa, Sigeru. 1980. Complex Verb and the Lexicon. Ph.
D. dissertation. University of Arizona.

Moortgat, Michael. 1981. Subcategoization and the notion
'lexical head'. <u>Linguistics</u> <u>in</u> <u>Netherlands</u>.
Amsterdam: North Holland.

----------. 1984. Fregean Principle on the metarules.
<u>Proceedings</u> <u>of</u> <u>NELS</u> 14.306-325. Amherst, Mass.: GLSA,
University of Massachusetts.

Morita, Yoshiyuki. 1981. <u>Nihongo</u> <u>no</u> <u>Hassoo</u>. Tokyo:
Toozyu-sha.

Nanni, Debbie. 1980. On the surface syntax of constructions
with <u>easy</u>type adjectives. <u>Language</u> 56.568-581.

Nishio, Toraya. 1961. Doosi-renyookei no meisika ni kansuru
iti-koosatu. <u>Kokugogaku</u> 43.60-81.

----------. 1976. Zoogohoo to ryakugohoo. <u>Nihongo-kooza</u>,
vol.4. Tokyo: Taisyuukan.

Nishio and Miyajima. 1971. <u>Doosi</u> <u>Keiyoosi</u> <u>Yooreisyuu</u>.
Tokyo: Kokuritu Kokugo Kenkyuusyo.

Okutsu, Keiichiroo. 1975. Fukugoo-meisi no seisei-bunpoo.
<u>Kokugogaku</u> 101.19-34.

----------. 1983. Bunpoo no yure. <u>Nihongogaku</u> 2. Tokyo:
Meiji-syoin.

Pawley, Andrew. 1980. On meeting a language that defies
description in ordinary terms. A paper prepared for the
Kivung Congress of the Linguistic Society of Papua New
Guinea, Lae.

Pesetsky, David. 1983. Morphology and logical form. ms.
University of Southern California.

Pranka, Paula M. 1983. Syntax and Word Formation. Ph. D.
dissertation. MIT.

Riemsdijk, H. C. Van. 1980. The case of German adjectives. *University of Massachusetts Occasional Papers* 6.148-173

Roeper, Thomas. 1983. Implicit thematic roles in the lexicon and syntax. ms. University of Massachusetts.

Roeper, T. and Siegel, M. 1978. A lexical transformation for verbal compounds. *Linguistic Inquiry* 9.148-173.

Sadock, Jerrold M. 1980. Noun incorporation in Greenlandic: a case of syntactic word formation. *Language* 56.300-319.

----------. 1983a. Linguistics as anatomy, or against strict modularity in grammar. ms. University of Chicago.

----------. 1983b. West Greenlandic clitic cline. ms. University of Chicago.

----------. 1984. A proposal for the treatment of noun incorporation. ms. University of Chicago.

Saito, Mamoru. 1982. Case marking in Japanese. ms. MIT.

----------. 1983. Comments on the papers on generative syntax. *Studies in Generative Grammar and Language Acquisition*. ed. by Y. Otsu et al. Tokyo: International Christian University.

Sapir, Edward. 1921. *Language*. New York: Harcourt, Brace and World.

Schachter, Paul. 1981. Lovely to look at. *Linguistic Analysis* 7.431-448.

Selkirk, Elizabeth. 1982. *The Syntax of Words*. (LI Monograph 7.) Cambridge, Mass.: MIT Press.

Siegel, Dorothy. 1973. Nonsources of unpassives. in J. Kimball ed. *Syntax and Semantics* 2. New York: Seminar Press.

----------. 1974. Topic in English Morphology. Ph. D. dissertation. MIT.

Shibatani, Masayosi. 1978. *Nihongo no Bunseki*. Tokyo: Taisyuukan.

Shibatani, M and Cotton, C. 1976/7. Double nominative construction. *Papers in Japanese Linguistics* 5.261-277.

Sugioka, Yoko. 1982. On the status of a verbal suffix -suru in Japanese. Unpublished paper. University of Chicago.

Sugioka, Y. and Lehr, R. 1983. Adverbial -ly as an inflectional affix. CLS Parasession on Interplay of Phonology, Morphology, and Syntax. Chicago: Chicago Linguistic Society. 293-300.

Tamura, Suzuko. 1968. Nihongo no tadoosi no kibookei/kanookei to zyosi. Kyooiku Kenkyuusyo Kiyoo 261-277. Tokyo: Waseda University.

Tonoike, Sigeo. 1975/6. The case ordering hypothesis. Papers in Japanese Linguistics 4.191-208.

Vance, Timothy J. 1979. Nonsense-word experiments in phonology and their application to Rendaku in Japanese. Ph. D. dissertation. University of Chicago.

Vergnaud, J. R. 1973. Formal properties of lexical derivations. Quarterly progress report of RLE, no. 108.279-287. MIT.

Wasow, Thomas. 1977. Transformation and the lexicon. Formal Syntax. ed. by P. Cullicover, et al. New York: Academic Press.

----------. 1980. Major and minor rules in lexical grammar. Lexical Grammar. ed. by T. Hoekstra, et al. Dordrecht: Foris.

Williams, Edwin. 1981. On the notions 'lexically related' and 'head of a word'. Linguistic Inquiry 12.245-274.

----------. 1981. Argument structure and morphology. Linguistic Review 1.81-114.

Yoshida, Kanehiko. 1971. Gendaigo Jodoosi no Si-teki Kenkyuu. Tokyo: Meiji-syoin.

Zwicky, Arnold, M. 1977. On clitics. Bloomington, Ind.: Indiana University Linguistic Club.

----------. 1978. Arguing for constituents. CLS 14.503-512. Chicago: Chicago Linguistic Society.

----------. 1982. An expanded view of morphology in the syntax-phonology interface. Preprints for the 13th International Congress of Linguists, Tokyo.

Zwicky, A. and Pullum G. 1983. Cliticization versus inflection: English n't. Language 59.502-513.

For Product Safety Concerns and Information please contact our EU
representative GPSR@taylorandfrancis.com
Taylor & Francis Verlag GmbH, Kaufingerstraße 24, 80331 München, Germany

www.ingramcontent.com/pod-product-compliance
Lightning Source LLC
Chambersburg PA
CBHW071822300426
44116CB00009B/1406